HUMPTY DUMPTY WAS PUSHED

a novel

MARC BLATTE

Book Cover: Erolli
Interior Design: Nonon Tech & Design

ISBN: 978-0-578-88056-3

Library of Congress Cataloguing in Publication Data:
Blatte, Marc, 1951 - Humpty Dumpty was Pushed: a novel / by Marc Blatte. - 1st ed. p.cm
1. Hip-hop-Fiction. 2. New York (N.Y.) - Fiction. I. Title.
PS3601.L395H86 2009
813'.6-dc22

2008024301

I dedicate this book to:
My loveboid, who's song is sooo sweet. Multi-million selling Bronx author, Evan Hunter, aka Ed McBain, for sharing the secret of his success, "I always finish what I start" with me when I was seventeen. The affection with which they were spoken and the rightness of their meaning will remain one of the greatest gifts of my life.
Scholar, conductor, teacher, short-lived Director of the National Endowment for the Arts and long-time friend Mike Hammond for insisting that I employ a system of thought that emphasizes the connectedness of seemingly small, insignificant events to large, significant outcomes.

IF YOU TELL THE TRUTH
YOU DON'T HAVE TO REMEMBER ANYTHING...
Mark Twain

Table of Contents

1

When Scholar showed up at the studio and threw ten Gs in cash down on the automated faders of the classic forty-eight channel Neve mixing board, Biz knew there was no way out of the deal. His cousin towered over him, lips in overdrive and cranking like a jungle groove at 180 bpm underneath his scruffy mustache-goatee. This man with the tattoos and the rock-hard physique, which only a prison gym could create, was on a mission, yo! As manager of his group, Proof Positive, he was gonna "blow up extra, extra large and be the bigges' on the planet. Hear me, bro? More bigger 'n Biggie Smalls, Snoop, Jay Z, all of 'em."

Biz had already tried to blow Scholar off more times than he could count, but his cousin never took no for an answer. "No" was a one-syllable excuse, a free ticket to ask for the same thing again. Scholar saw him as a convenient step on his ladder to wealth and fame, a little man with big connections. Biz had said he needed "stupid green" to get the project moving forward, and now here Scholar was, raining mad cash down on the console. Wasn't no big thing.

"Yo, Little Man," Scholar said, after all the bills had left his hands, falling in a thick pile of twenties and fifties. "There it is. Make it happen."

Biz didn't really want to produce Proof Positive, even though Scholar was his cousin on his mama's side and she was always bugging him to help his cuz break into the "reckit bidness." Biz was well connected, re-spected, and rolling in the dough; he didn't need this shit. Scholar was a royal pain in the butt. But truth be told, Scholar and his Proof guys scared the living shit out of him.

Despite his big rep in the hip-hop game, Biz was no ghetto thug. He was a gentle man with the gift of crafting multi-platinum hits. So what if, way back in the day, his grandmother had given birth to twins who gave birth to boys who were forever linked by blood as cousins? Biz could run away from Scholar, which he had done many times, but he couldn't hide. No matter how much he insisted, his mama could not help but give his whereabouts to her nosy sister, Florice, who, of course, passed it on to her lazy, devious, violently twisted, criminal son.

As long as Biz could remember, Scholar had always beat on, bullied, and ridiculed him. Calling him Little Man, as he had just done, was just one example, as if Biz were still some nappy-headed kid. Always disrespecting him. Always disrespecting everyone, come to think of it. Scholar had not changed one iota from the time he came out of his mama, screaming for her succulent, nourishing titty in exchange for doing what? Crying and screaming?

He was supposedly a man now. But a man took care of his business. He worked, and he worked hard. A man didn't burden other people with his problems. Scholar was a baby in the body of a man—an adult still fixated on finding the big titty, something that would deliver everything he needed in exchange for as little work as possible. As if such a thing existed.

At the moment, to Scholar's distorted way of thinking, hip-hop was that big generous titty. In his dreams, he could taste it. In his day-to-day living, he was always thinking up ways to get his mouth on it and start sucking. The way Biz saw it, Scholar's dreams and schemes were all a big waste of time. Scholar was destined to be what he was now and always would be—a small-time drug dealer, hustler, and thief who ran with a posse of thugs from the Far Rock PJs. Thieving, stealing, and robbing and shit—a plague on the neighborhood, a disgrace to African-American manhood.

Biz remembered the first time Scholar had been sent upstate, barely eighteen years old, for assault with a deadly weapon. His aunt was inconsolable and it broke his own mama's heart to see her sister in such a bad way. As far as he was concerned, they should have locked Scholar's ass down tight, right then and there, and thrown away the key. But no, it didn't happen that way. Some shyster had gotten him out, after only three years of doing time. The result was that Scholar was now in his face, throwing money down, insisting that he "step up."

But, Biz had to admit that his predicament was of his own making. In one of his many attempts to stop Scholar from bothering him all the time, about taking Proof Positive into the studio, he had told him, plain and simple, that if he could come up with fifteen grand cash, he'd make a demo of Proof. He knew that no one in his right mind paid that kind of money for a demo, even if he was loaded. But, in a moment of supreme denial, he had forgotten that Scholar qualified as someone not in his right mind. And now, what could he say? His insane cousin had shown up with the money. Bidness was bidness. Word was bond. He had made a deal, and he was locked into it, and, truth be told, he was terrified not to go ahead with it.

Scholar was staring at him with that penitentiary, who's-the-player-now look, which implied, "Don't you dare fuck with me, bitch, or, blood or no blood, I'll waste your ass." Biz knew the look well. Half the kids from his neighborhood had it. If prison did that to young men, he would do everything he could to stay out. He was a lover, not a fighter. The women loved him. He was suave, and he was sweet. For the ladies he was a treat: light cocoa, tall, lean, eyes to die for—made to be seen. Yup, Biz had it goin' on. All he wanted to do was make his music, smile, and spread joy.

So when Scholar said, "When you gonna make it happen?" he knew what his response had to be, and, as emasculated as it made him feel, he gave it. "Yo, Scholar, you da man." He waited and then added, "I got to edit Jah Ray E all day tomorrow. He down with the Elektrik crew."

The pause obviously irritated Scholar, who probably read it as reluctance and a bit of defiance. "I don't wanna hear when you cain't do it, Little Man," he said, "just tell me when it's on." He wasn't playing.

Biz, being from the hood, had his radar on perpetual scan for things to fear and avoid. And, right now, the signal activating his fight-or-flee instinct was set to broadcast quality. "How 'bout we put down vocals tomorrow night at Sound RX Scholar? 'Round ten. At 40 Duane Street. Fourth floor. Say you with me."

"Bet, yo."

The Proof was hanging on the sidewalk practicing rhymes as Scholar got out of the beat-up Ford Crown Victoria from the car service in Far Rock. They greeted him with high fives and love. "I tolt you my cuz was gonna take us next level," he said, grinning.

"Word!" their mouths chimed in unison. "It's a fait accompli, my brothers."

The group didn't know shit about French phrases, but they knew the gist of what it meant. Scholar's cousin was a playa and producer/writer for the owner of the all time biggest record label in hip-hop, Sunn Volt. And Biz, well, what could they say? They had just seen his ass on BET. The boy was lookin' good. It was slick, the way he bigged up his latest joint. He was the pride of the hood, no doubt about it. The homeboy with the Midas touch. They was goin' into the studio with Biz, yo! That shit was money in the bank.

While his cuz was cruising on back on the BQE, Biz wondered what the fuck he had just gotten himself into, knowing that a night in the studio with Scholar and his amateur crew would drive him crazy. To make himself feel better, he tried thinking of all the hours he'd spent with thugs just like Proof, who went on to go double platinum. There were quite a few . . . well, at least one. Maybe. Then he rationalized that ten thousand cash—with another five on the way—was a lot of money. Then he had a temporary moment of clarity. He didn't need it. That was plain and simple. It occurred to him that his willingness to accept the gig was all about deep fear. With all his success, his connections and his fame, when it came to his cousin, he was still a frightened little boy waiting for another inevitable smack upside the head.

MARC BLATTE

2

"I know this guy...or someone who looks a lot like him," Black Sallie Blue Eyes said to no one in particular, referring to the over-sized corpse lying on the pavement in the big outdoor parking lot at 22nd Street, just west of Fifth Avenue. He inspected the two entry wounds in the chest and another one in the back of the head.

"Over at Starbucks last week. I remember him being very particular about his coffee." He sighed then glanced away to admire the cornices of the old buildings adjacent to the parking lot. Their beauty and graceful design soothed him for a moment, taking his mind off the bloody mess in front of him. "Somebody run a check on those two cars left in here," he said. "I want to know who owns them and what they were doing tonight."

"It's in the works, Sal," Teddy Schwartz said. "Hey, what do you make of the bright yellow socks? Everything the dead guy's wearing is black, except for those. You think the guy's a Latin King?"

"Yeah, and I'm a Saudi Prince. Gimme a break, Ted." Sallie said to his twenty-something, Samson-before-the haircut, partner.

"Look at that stupid bling the guy's got around his neck and that whack-ass belt buckle with the leather pants. It doesn't fit. I'd give odds this guy's no native son. Everything about him says 'off the boat and not the Staten Island Ferry.'" Sallie was now on the ground and up close and personal with the dead man. "This guy's no Latin Lover, either. Unh-uh, are you, big guy? More like Frankenstein. The body type, his dark coloring and facial features—I'd say Central Europe."

Teddy followed Sallie as he moved quickly from the body toward the third member of their team, Jackie Gleason. Handsome brother, born and raised in the South Bronx and first ever from the large, hard working Gleason family to graduate college, a good one and in the neighborhood too, Fordham U. "Hey, Gleason, what's the victim's name?"

Gleason examined what he was holding in his hand. "Says on his license he's Pashko Gazivoda. Lives over on Pelham Parkway."

"Now we're talking! See, Teddy boy? With all due modesty, it fits." He turned to take another look at the dead man. "I like you, Pashko. You're eccentric—a real individual. I admire your geeky outfit with the yellow socks and the bling. I wouldn't get caught dead in it even though you did. It's all good. I like someone who's got personal style. That's important. So let me ask you something, Pashko, you mind? Okay, what the fuck were you doing here on a Saturday night at four o'clock in the morning?" He turned and walked about twenty feet to the sidewalk. Peering east, he focused on a hanging sign. "Were you partying at the Kiki Club?" He glanced over his shoulder. "Hey, Teddy," he hollered. "Get Neil Weinstein on the phone. He's the owner of the Kiki. Maybe he knows this Pashko."

Without waiting for a response, Sallie marched over to the corpse again. "Pashko, my man, do you know Neil? I bet you do." Right on cue, Teddy handed him the cell phone. "Hey, Neil, I hate to be bothering you this early in the morning, but I'm out in the parking lot by your club. There's a kid here named Pashko. He's been shot up pretty bad." Sallie nodded at the police forensic team that arrived on the scene. "Yeah, Neil, I'm afraid so, about as dead as a guy with half a face and his brains blown out can get. Was the kid ever in any kind of trouble, 'cause it looks like whoever did the dirty deed wanted him really dead really bad."

Sallie eyed the photographer, who snapped pictures of Pashko from several angles. "I'm real sorry, Neil. This Pashko…his license says he lives up over on Pelham Parkway. My guys and me are going on over there now. We'll talk again later."

Black Sallie Blue Eyes was one of New York's most decorated cops. The name on his Italian birth certificate and his American passport was Salvatore Fortunato Messina. The moniker "Black Sallie Blue Eyes" was bestowed upon him by Joe "Turtle" Salvo, a long deceased numbers man Sal had brought down when he was doing undercover. Joe told the young detective the name fit for two reasons. "The first is obvious, as plain as the nose on my face, Sal. It's physical. How many of us guinea bastards you know got ice blue eyes? The second is for your hair color and personality to go with it. Black."

To prove their point, the cops had the bookmaker on a wire telling Al "Snake Eyes" Ricci, "Don't bother trying to spin your bullshit on Sal, he knows the color of the world we live in, Snake, and it ain't rosy. It's more like what you see when you get your head shoved half way up your asshole."

"That's fuckin' bleak, Joe." Snake hissed.

"And another thing", Joe said "The fuckin' kid is unflappable." The silence that followed tipped Turtle to the fact that Snake wasn't tracking what he meant too good.

"In other words, Snake," Turtle explained, "The kid's got balls to the floor and ice water running through his veins."

Sal was built tight, wiry, and had this pit bull aggressiveness about him. He worked out, ran marathons— New York, Boston, San Francisco—and he played b-ball. From three point range he was killer, and unlike many small guys he wasn't afraid to take it to the hoop even when it meant he'd get bounced by the big guys underneath.

He also had the gift or as some guys called it "he could smell the gun" which, simply put, meant he would know what you were gonna do before you did it.

Fred Kelly, his first partner, explained it like this. "When we were rookies we stumbled on a robbery in progress. The perp was a kid, maybe eighteen if that, had just held up a liquor store and was on his way out, gun still in hand. Sal gets out of the car, fucking cowboy that he is, got his drawn too. The kid points his gun right at Sal and is muttering some kind of nonsense, to tell you the truth it may have been in Spanish, I don't know. I got my gun on the little motherfucker ready to put pieces of him all over the sidewalk then I hear Sal. He says, 'Put the gun down, Freddy,' talking to me like I'm the fuckin' criminal' I say, 'What?' He says 'Freddy please, put the gun down. This young man doesn't want to shoot anybody.' I look over at Sal and he's looking at the kid all sympathetic like. Sal then puts his gun down. And the fuck of it is he looks completely relaxed like la-de-da aren't we having a nice day! Then he says, 'Please young man. You're scaring me. Please, put the gun down so nobody gets hurt.' Then he slowly starts walking to the kid. I swear, the kid put the gun down. We cuffed him and he came peacefully, no problem. I couldn't believe it. When we had a chance to talk it over, Sal said that when he looked at the kid's face he didn't see the face of a killer. I was like 'what the fuck does that mean?'

He says, 'I looked into his eyes and I got to tell you, Fred, I knew the kid just wasn't a killer.'

'Okay,' I said. 'Whatever you say.' And that's where we left it. The crazy thing is that when we questioned the kid he told us he never intended to use the weapon and he gave it up because the way Sal spoke to him, 'like a man, showed him respect.'

'Now, you could say the incident proves nothing; big deal, Sal took a chance, lived to tell, he's one lucky prick— but we found ourselves over and over in these situations where we had to make a determination to use force or not and every time whichever way Sal called it, he was right. It was like a joke, but it was funny scary. When a man can look in someone's face and predict his behavior, when he's got a record a mile long of getting it right every time, there's something to it. That's what makes Sal special."

"A couple of years after we started working together, I heard about this guy Paul Ekman, in this class I was taking over at John Jay. He studies facial expressions. Works with the CIA, FBI, joint terrorism forces and such. What he does is teach how the muscles in the face telegraph emotions like fear, anger, disgust, surprise, sadness, and happiness. I sent him a letter, told him all about Sal's thing. Long story short, when Sal went out to Frisco for the marathon, he stopped by and got tested by Ekman. Guess what? Seems Sal and the professor had been using the same indicators and techniques. Example: like when we were interrogating perps, I noticed Sal never did the tough guy intimidation thing. According to Ekman, that's old school shit. What Sal does is he gets a flow going and all the time he's studying the perp's face. You now how these wise asses do, just love to talk about themselves. Blah, blah blah, they think they're getting over on Sal. But just the opposite is going down, the bastards are giving Sal information he's gonna nail them with, which of course being the punks they are, they're oblivious to. It's kind of like Sallie's a magician, taking their socks off without touching their shoes."

The drive north took them exactly forty-five minutes, including a breakfast pit-stop at a greasy spoon somewhere off the Cross Bronx, from the time they left Manhattan to the time they pulled into a parking spot right in front of Pashko's five story, red brick apartment building on Pelham Parkway. When the super buzzed them in, Sallie muttered, "Amazing, two miracles in one day. We found a parking spot and the super in less than ten minutes. Maybe it's a sign." The trio headed to the elevator and up to the fifth floor. From there the super led them down a wide spotless hallway to Pashko's apartment. The door was cracked open.

Sallie wasted no time. With his voice amped and his gun drawn, he pounded on the door. "Police. Anybody home?

A heavyset woman with runny mascara and a tear- streaked face pulled the door wider. "Thank God, you're here. Come in. Come in." Several people were sitting around a dining room table. From their ages and the strikingly similar "I'm not from here, I'm from very far away" look on their faces, Sallie guessed they were the victim's family.

"Would you like some coffee?" their host apparent asked, motioning for them to follow her into the apartment.

"Whatever you have would be very much appreciated," Sal said.

He and his team were ushered into a sunken living room. An oversized couch facing a monstrous-sized home entertainment system dominated the space. It reminded Sal of the monolith minus the monkeys in Kubrick's 2001. A coffee table between the couch and TV was piled high with all kinds of Play Station paraphernalia. The walls were slathered with countless posters of gangsta rappers, sex kittens, basketball players, and fast cars.

"What a dick pit." Jackie whispered, eying the adolescent décor. "This place is giving me pimples."

As the sad-eyed, middle-aged woman shuffled to the kitchen for refreshments, the rest of the group carried their chairs into the living room and placed them directly across from where the detectives were sitting.

"So?" Sallie said, peering at the rapt faces of his audience. It was an open-ended comment. He figured someone would run with it.

A young man dressed like a spokesman for Source Magazine started the ball rolling. In perfectly accented Bronxese, he said, "I'm Alex Gazivoda. I live here with my cousins Vooko Congoli and Pashko Gazivoda. Her there in the kitchen is my moms. This man next to me is my pops. Those two over there is my aunt and uncle." He pointed to each in turn.

Sallie noted that the way he had pronounced aunt rhymed with want, not can't. "Right. So what is everybody doing here?"

"This morning when I get up, my two cousins aren't here. I try calling their cells, but nobody picks up. I'm like 'yo, this is weird.' So I call my folks and they call my uncle and aunt and everybody comes over to wait. And now you guys show up. So what's going on?"

Being a native New Yorker, Sallie did the New York thing. He answered the question with a question. "When was the last time you were in touch with them?"

"When they left for work, 'round six last night."

"Oh, yeah, and where do they work?"

"Downtown in this club called Kiki. They're security."

"Tough job."

"Yeah, they take care of business."

Sallie glanced at Ted and Jackie and then at the expectant faces of the family. He rubbed his hands together. "How about the other folks?" Mr. Slick addressed the group in an unidentifiable language that sounded nothing like the immigrant languages the detective was familiar with. Whatever had just been said prompted a lot of commotion. The detectives were blasted with a cacophony of anxious voices.

"Where are these people from?"

"They're from Serbia, but they're speaking Albanian. You know Kosovo. We're from that part of the world."

Sal had read about it. A former Yugoslav republic, home to genocide, unspeakable violence and cultural enmity that went back over seven hundred years.

"I see." Sal said. "And your cousins? They're from over there too."

"They were born there but the families moved here when they were teenagers."

"They must have seen a lot of awful stuff."

Alex averted Sal's eyes, spoke softly, "We all did. It was like hell there. We're lucky to be alive."

Sal gave an empathetic "I'm sorry," then a clipped, "You said they left last night and nobody's heard of them since."

"That's right." The cousin's voice emerged. It had an edge to it, as if it were Sallie's fault Pashko and Vooko had disappeared.

Sallie rubbed the back of his neck. "What were they wearing?"

"They was dressed in all black, 'cept for theys socks was yellow. Pashko has this gold medallion."

That confirmed the worst of his fears. "You haven't heard from either of them?"

"Word."

Sallie glanced at Alex. He'd broken news like this maybe two hundred times and it always left him grieving for the victim, for the family, for himself, for mankind. "Young man, would you mind stepping outside with me?"

When Sallie sprung up from the couch, everyone but the detectives rose in unison, old world style. He'd bet that future generations wouldn't be as polite. On this side of the ocean, respect for others was as hard to find as an innocent defendant.

"Please, sit down," he said to everyone in the room. He held his palm in a practiced gesture that expressed humility and gravity. "Excuse me. We'll be back in a minute." He led Alex outside of the apartment where they could speak privately, and then waited.

Alex jammed his hands into his pockets and lowered his eyes before lifting them again. "Are my cousins in some kind of trouble or something?"

"What do you mean?" Sallie asked, in a concerned manner.

"Like, did they do something stupid? You know, mess somebody up?"

"Why would you say that?"

"I know where they work can get kind of crazy."

"No, not that I know of." Sallie reached into his jacket pocket. "I need to show you something that may belong to your cousin." He pulled out a plastic bag and held it up so Alex could see what was inside.

"Oh, shit."

"Is that your cousin's license?"

"Yeah." Instantly, Alex was trembling.

Sallie gripped his shoulder and squeezed. "Try to stay calm, son. Your family needs you right now. Take a few deep breaths. It'll help keep you focused." He stepped back, in case the kid needed some space. "If that's Pashko, which I assume it is, he's passed on. We found him in a parking lot near the Kiki."

The kid was breathing deeply, as Sallie had instructed, but it wasn't helping. He was about to do the European thing, cry his eyes out. Sal was embarrassed. The kid had been here long enough to know tears were for babies on this side of the Atlantic. He moved closer and gave him a hug and held the young man who continued sobbing for several minutes. "Hey, Alex, I guess that deep breathing didn't do it for you," he said.

Alex managed a weak imitation of a laugh. "I'm okay."

"Now, do you know why anybody would want to hurt your cousin?"

Alex shook his head.

"Okay, we're going to go back inside and you're going to have to break the news. I'll be standing next to you. While you're doing that, my detectives are going to take a look around the apartment. Right?"

"Yeah, sure, but what about my other cuz, Vooko? He was with Pashko last night. Where's he at?"

"I don't know, but I'll let you know as soon as I do."

They went back inside. Sal stood reverently beside Alex as he broke the news. Wails, grief, arms reaching out to one another for comfort. In deference Sal asked the family if they minded if his detectives took a look around.

No one had a problem with it.

Jack and Ted hit the bathrooms first, walls dirty, tubs grimy and toilet edged with slime. The corroding medicine cabinets were overflowing with every men's grooming product ever advertised on ESPN. They moved quickly, found nothing, then went on to the bedrooms.

Jackie and Ted didn't have to guess whose room was whose. The guys made it easy. Vooko and Alex had massive silver medallions nailed onto their doors that identified each occupant. The two private bedrooms were equally disastrous. Each one was dominated by a king-sized mattress on the ground that was covered in mismatched sheets and pillowcases. All floor space was occupied by piles of underwear, socks, shirts, pants and sweats, and wall space was taken by an assortment of posters that paid tribute to the same Gangster Rapper lifestyle that graced the living room.

Pashko's room didn't have any of the bling broadcasting the name of it's occupant but it did have a neon sign on the wall where the letters P A S H K O glowed in a cool pink and blue among posters of female hard bodies. Clothes were thrown all over the black sheets on the king size four-poster bed and the orange shag rug. A floor to ceiling mirror reflected the anarchy, making it look twice as disgusting.

Jackie stole a quick look at his reflection, then went right to a laptop perched on a small freestanding bookshelf overflowing with car and gun magazines.

"I'm gonna take this with us, Teddy."

Ted was rummaging through piles of sweaters and running suits on the closet floor.

"I don't see why not, partner."

"You find anything of interest, Ted?"

"Nothing, Jackie."

"So we good?"

"I wouldn't say good, Jackie." Teddy stood and wiped his hands on his jeans. "Good would be a bath in a tub of Lysol."

3

Spahiu Congoli—the name on his passport, aka Vooko, his street name—came to the Bronx happy to be alive from war torn, piss poor Kosovo, exactly two years after the Serbs started their rape/kill, rape/maim, kill/kill "ethnic cleansing" of his people. "The Bronx," is what his parents called it, but Vooko liked to say he was a "B-boy from the Boogie Down." It had a ring of freedom to it, of danger and adventure. Not quite like the real-life shit he'd seen back in his hometown of Pec, when he was running guns to freedom fighters. Back there, when he got in the mood for a little fun, he could actually shoot up some bad guys, which he had done on one or two occasions, or wreak novel forms of mayhem on the enemies of his people, ditto.

That kind of thing didn't really play in New York, but he loved watching the fantasy of it on TV, and he had a lot fun wasting thugs, punks, and assassins on his PlayStation 2. The nonstop screen action reminded him of home, only the shit that went on back there was for real. Some days he missed being a next-level badass motherfucker. God, did he detest law and order! Like the affable fellow who rated movies on Channel 13, he gave it a big "two thumbs way down." It just didn't play like chaos and terror.

Not that he was completely out of the terror game. If one of his uncles had troubles with a worker at his restaurant or certain issues needed clearing up with the landlord, Vooko was the man. Some kind of bullshit was always going down with his various relatives in small businesses, who also had plenty of friends in need of a little extra help now and then, so he had a small, steady income as a "crisis counselor." Most of the time, he didn't have to do much to smooth things out. He would just show up. Somehow, being in a room with all six-feet six-inches and 270 pounds of him, with his fierce, mean, butt-ugly face breathing down on the folks was enough to make most of them see the unreasonableness of their position pronto. Every once in a while, some guy would try to be a hero and act as if Vooko couldn't intimidate him. This was always a mistake; dialogue was not Vooko's forte.

Whiny-ass businessmen annoyed him, especially when they were doing what the brothers called "fronting"—acting as though they had everything under control. That was when he would typically lose patience and do his Eastern European shock-the-motherfucker-shitless sort of physical assault, delivered with lightning speed. It had strong powers of persuasion.

So far, he had never had to go beyond his initial attack before the enemy of his client would become reasonable. He saw this rate of success as both good and bad. Good because the violence was minimal and bad because he sometimes wanted to take it next level and to feel that nostalgic, near death, adrenaline rush that he used to get sometimes back in the day in the old country. when he'd managed to stay alive against all odds.

Weekends, he worked the door at the Kiki Club in Manhattan, a job he'd gotten through his cuz, Pashko. On the club circuit, Vooko was known as "the guy who lets you in for a coffee." Not just any kind, though. It had to be Starbucks. Starbucks Sumatra always gave him the nice jitters. More specifically, it had to be a double latte with a touch of hot cocoa—and made with steamed soymilk, thank you, not that white shit that comes from overmedicated cows.

Vooko was good at his job of controlling the line. He had a feel for the mood of the crowd. He could sense early on whether it was going to be laid-back or off-the-hook hard to control.

Last Saturday night had gotten way off the hook right away. There were the usual gangs of bridge and tunnel kids in for a night on the town, in riotous-behavior mode and acting like antiseptic mall-rat versions of ghetto punks. He had come to think of these kids as "the idiots," like the title character in Dostoyevsky's novel. (He'd read the Cliff Notes for a book report way back in high school.) How did they do it, he wondered, as he watched the regular mooks patiently waiting their turn for entrance. Who would give any of these rejects a job? What work could they possibly do that had enough earning potential to pay for night after night at the Kiki?

All kinds flocked to the Kiki, of course. The ones who walked straight in were the Wall Street types—Ivy league, MBA money guys who liked the gangster rep of the club scene there: candy cars, quality ass, and drugs. At first, Vooko mistook MBA for NBA, and it threw him, because not one of these guys was over six-four, and most of them were unfit and white. But it didn't take him long to get it. They might not be able to sink free throws at eighty-five percent, but they didn't need to; they could buy a whole team of guys who could. He liked these guys. He could relate to them. They had the look of predators, like the militia leaders in his old country.

Vooko had learned early on that no big club would have any cachet without celebrities, and usually the place was full of them. It had taken him a long time to understand about the celebrity phenomenon, and he still wasn't all that clear on it. His bosses had told him point-blank that anybody who "looked" famous got special treatment. He had nothing against being extra nice to anyone. In his former life, he had made the effort, but it was always because he knew the big shots personally and respected them, or he didn't know them but knew they could easily kill him or have him killed. Not like here with all the wanker posers and their sleek, useless entourages.

He attributed his ignorance of this phenomenon to the fact that he had come from a war-ravaged piss-bucket of a country. In the town of his birth, there were no celebrities. You stood about as much chance of finding a two-headed goat. There was no urgent need for media hype, because there was no media left that mattered. Over the years, rival militias had shot and shelled the movie theater to ruins; the printed page, when you could find one, was best used as toilet paper; and the intermittent electric service made television rare and unreliable. Not having had much exposure to the images that created hype, Vooko just couldn't get that into it.

On most nights, things at the Kiki Club in Manhattan ran pretty smoothly. Altercations were generally between regular patrons. The fights were always smalltime disturbances that flared brightly for a second and then fizzled—two guys mixing it up over some girl or two girls yanking each other's hair out over a guy. Sometimes it was about drugs—somebody feeling ripped off or scammed.

Heated words might get exchanged, and maybe some minor physical thing would go down, nothing big. Vooko expected these things to happen and he took them in stride. He was a pro. As the man who works the line on weekend nights, his job was to keep the peace. It was all about business. Within the course of an evening he expected that there would be a couple of times when a few potential patrons might get bitchy with him, because they had to wait too long or because somebody got in ahead of them who they didn't think was as hip as they were. He could deal with that; that's what he was paid to do.

He could understand the frustration, too. In this country, there was competition for everything, even for a place in line on a Saturday night. From what he could see, Americans were not happy campers. In fact, just the opposite, they were jumping over their own asses trying to get ahead, and unlike him, they were not enjoying the anxiety and stress.

Right now, as he lay in a hospital bed in a semi delirious state, scenes from the last Saturday played incessantly in his head. The night was one for the record books. Extra fucked up and out of control. Some hip-hop record company had launched a new act—a young punk called Five Star, as in five-star general. He had no problem with African- Americans specifically; on the whole, he found them as inconsiderate, self-centered, and offensive as every other ethnic group in his new homeland. It was just that, when the additional ghetto thugs on the Elektrik label's guest list were squeezed into the already packed club, the waiting time to get in grew from about forty minutes to ninety minutes, which is a long time for anyone to stand in line to get into a club. That night, a crowd of about three hundred people had lined 21st Street, and they were real restless.

The thought of last Saturday's incident outside the Kiki still gave Vooko the creeps, and now, lying awake in his hospital bed, he had plenty of time to relive every second of it. There was this kid who had been trying to get into the club without waiting in line. He had made an instant impression, because he looked more upscale than your typical idiot; he was duded up in Armani, not the low-end Emporio threads. The cashmere V-neck he was wearing probably went for three grand all by itself.

But something was obviously wrong, the kid was so high, he had the shakes. He sidled up way too close and, in this nasty way, said he had to see if his sister was inside. Vooko had to give the kid an A for originality. Ninety-nine out of a hundred of the bozos like him said they wanted to see their girl inside. Vooko considered the request. He looked at the line going around the block, then back at Mr. Armani. It was the worst time of night to deliver a favor.

"It's too busy," he told the kid, motioning for him to stand back a little.

Right as he did this, one of the regulars, a Wall Street guy, sauntered past him, straight into the club, without standing in line. The kid was outraged. "What the fuck is that? What the fuck is that?" repeating it, as if

Vooko hadn't heard him screeching in his ear the first time. "You just told me everybody has to wait in line. You just told me everybody has to wait in line. That fuckin' guy just walked in. He just fuckin' walked right into the place!"

Vooko didn't want to aggravate the situation. "Please, take it easy. You'll get your turn."

"Take it easy? You take it easy! I'll get my turn? You just let that preppy ass-wipe walk into the place. Don't bullshit me, motherfucker. Don't bullshit me."

Vooko had always liked this word "motherfucker." It was used in all sorts of contexts—rage, for instance, as in "Don't fuck with me, motherfucker." Or playfulness, as in "Don't fuck with me, motherfucker." It all depended on how it was said. It was a true American utility word. He loved it when a real tough guy was described as a "bad motherfucker." In fact, Vooko's greatest wish was to be a bad motherfucker. But the malevolent way the skinny kid had just called him "motherfucker" did not have the complimentary ring that befitted the type of motherfucker Vooko considered himself to be.

The kid needed an attitude adjustment. So, Vooko smiled. "Did you just call me a motherfucker, motherfucker?"

Then Armani went ballistic on him. "You think I'm not serious, shithead? Are you playing me? Are you playing me? Are you playing me?"

Two things happened after that. One of the most beautiful white girls Vooko had ever seen came out of the club and raced over to the kid. "What the fuck are you doing?" she said to him. Then she glanced at Vooko. "He's okay. He's coming in with me."

While all this was going on, the other outside bouncer— Vooko's boss, Bobby Martinez—told the kid and his supposed sister to stay right where they were. He had been monitoring the scene and didn't like what he was seeing. To him, they seemed like a security risk and he didn't want them in the club. He took Vooko aside. "The kid's on something. Send the little fucker home."

Bobby was running a power trip, but it was his show. Vooko was just the messenger. So, he went over to the couple and told them the bad news.

On hearing this, the kid looked at the girl and tried talking to her, but nothing came out of his mouth, and he started shaking so badly that Vooko half expected him to explode. Then, for some reason, he ran at Bobby, who had his back turned, jumped on his shoulders and bit down on his ear. Blood gushed everywhere. Bobby tried to defend himself, but Armani refused to give it up. Eventually, Bobby collapsed right there on the blacktop with the kid still on top of him—an elephant brought down by a well-dressed shrew.

Vooko couldn't believe his eyes. Not only was big Bobby down, but the little shit was standing over him screaming, "Get back up, bitch!"

Vooko ran over and clapped a chokehold on the kid, dragged him— half lifting him—forty feet into the parking lot next to the club, and slammed him against the wall. This seemed to settle him down some, but then the kid surprised Vooko with a head-butt. Vooko heard a crunch and felt a blinding jolt of pain. He grabbed his nose to protect it, at which point the kid used one of Vooko's own standards on him…a kick to the groin. As he lay on the blacktop in a fetal position, the kid spat on him. "You want more, bitch? Who's your daddy? Who's your daddy?"

Vooko had a father who was at that moment probably watching TV in his apartment on Pelham Parkway. He remembered wondering what this 'who's your daddy?' meant. He also remembered hoping someone from security was aware of what was going on and would come over to help him out, because if someone didn't step in soon, the kid would probably kill him.

The one universal truth at the top of Vooko's list of universal truths was that the unexpected could always be expected to happen. What occurred next confirmed this. From out of nowhere, the kid's sister took off her shoe and smacked him on the head with the four-inch spike heel. While the girl was bashing his head, the kid spewed vomit all over him.

Where Vooko had gotten the strength, he didn't know, but he leaped up and palmed the beauty solidly in the solar plexus, just as he sometimes did while engaged in "crisis counseling." She had gone down gasping. Then he swung the kid's arm behind his back, yanked upward, and was immediately rewarded with a satisfying shriek.

That's when the cops had shown up.

The NYPD were consummate professionals. They separated Vooko and the kid and checked on the girl. Vooko had knocked the wind out of her, but she said she was okay. The cops asked for an ID; Vooko was in the process of showing the officers his driver's license, when the club owner, Neil Weinstein, arrived on the scene.

Clearly, the cops knew Neil well. He had been operating in the neighborhood for years. Neil told the cops that this was "the most fucked-up thing" he had ever seen, which was saying a lot, considering all the years he'd spent owning clubs. "Thank you for coming so quickly, officers. No one wants to press charges. The club will pay for any medical bills of the parties involved."

Within minutes, they all agreed that it was in everyone's best interest to call it a night. That was the last Vooko saw of the psycho kid and his sister as they pulled away in a silver Porsche.

With his nose still bleeding, he took one of those fleet cabs—with so little room in the back he could barely fit—to The Beth Israel Emergency Room. It was a slow night at the hospital, so it took only an hour before he had been checked in, examined, and X-rayed. As it turned out, it could have been a lot worse. His nose wasn't broken, and everything seemed to be in working order. Once he was out of Beth Israel, he got on his cell and called Pashko, who was working security inside the Kiki Club. Pashko told him to hop in a cab and stop by the club; they would live large for a couple hours and then take another cab home together.

That's exactly what they had done.

Going up the West Side Highway later that night, his bad-ass cousin and he had been feeling good. They talked it over and decided that compared to smuggling guns to Albanian patriots—past border patrols of maniacal Serb militias—the freak show with the kid and his sister had been a walk in the park. In fact, they agreed that, overall, life was pretty good. They looked alike and they liked how they looked. They lived together in their own three-bedroom over on Pelham Parkway, which they shared with their fashion- conscious American-born cuz, Alex. Thanks to him, they even dressed alike. He had turned both of them on to that "B-boy from the Boogie Down" flavor that they sported and the hip-hop speechifying that had become part of who they were. If you asked them, they would tell you they "was stylin,' yo, keepin' it real." They "was blood." Pashko said it all the time. "We stuck to each other like white on rice, yo. Twenty-four seven, I got his back, and he gots mine."

As they rode in comfort to their nice apartment with indoor plumbing and a working refrigerator, they discussed how the next morning, they would have breakfast at their favorite diner, where they would feast on international cuisine. Pashko would savor Canadian bacon and French toast and Vooko would wolf down a Greek omelet. Yes, the U.S. of A. was their country now and life was good, very good.

That altercation with skinny boy and his glamour-gal sister had been exactly one week ago. Now, seven short days later, Vooko's ass was strapped down in yet another hospital. In his drugged out state, he had no idea that this hospital was different from the one he'd visited before.

What he did remember through the fog of excruciating pain, shortness of breath, and delirium, was overhearing someone say "This guy's lucky to be alive." He assumed they meant him. Then his mind took him on a little journey where he heard shots being fired, and saw himself running to make his successful escape. He wondered what had happened to his beloved cousin Pashko....

Several hours later, Vooko felt a small pinch on his little toe. When he lifted his eyelids far enough to peek through his lashes, he found three sets of eyes staring into his. Mr. Muscles and the brother were around his age and the third guy—with jet-black hair and pale blue eyes—was older. Damn, he hated having people look down on him. He was used to it being the other way around. The older one asked, "How you doing, big guy?"

He felt awful, but he said what everyone in America always said. "Fine."

"Man, you don't look fine."

This was from the brother. Vooko eyed him with curiosity. The man was dressed in a relaxed sort of street outfit: a maroon t-shirt, khaki light-weight jacket with a NY Yankee baseball lid. His vibe was chill, too. He'd bet money the man was from the Boogie Down. In pain he shifted on the hard hospital bed and attempted to reach for a glass of water on the bed-side table. Trying not to wince took enormous self-control. He despised any show of weakness.

"What happen to you, Big Dogg?" Boogie Down asked. He reached for the water and held the glass.

Vooko sipped from the straw in the water glass. "Who're you? What you want?"

Muscles stepped closer. "We're detectives."

Immediately, Icy Blue Eyes jumped into the conversation, "You know, your cousin Pashko's dead."

Vooko fell back on the hard bed pillow and shut his eyes. He didn't know these men or if what they had just said was true, but it probably was. He steeled himself by remembering that this was not the first time someone close to him had died. He thought of his many relatives who had been marched into muddy fields and executed by militias. *Even here, in the land of light*, he thought, *the darkness follows us.*

"Why would someone want to kill your cousin?" Chill asked.

Will talking to them do any good? Will it bring Pashko back to life? Vooko opened his eyes and shook his head against the pillow. The move sent a shooting pain across his forehead causing him to wince.

"He was shot." Pale Eyes showed him a picture of Pashko's body. "We found him in the parking lot next to the Kiki."

Vooko turned his head and clamped his eyes tight against the image. He felt someone pinch his toe again. "What happened to you?"

He didn't even bother to check out which of the three wanted to know. "I remember nothin." He heard feet shuffling toward the door of his room. "We'll be back" one of them said.

Big fuckin' deal, he thought. *Pashko won't.*

A nurse came in.

"How much longer am I s'posed to be here for?" Vooko asked.

"Boy," the the nurse said with a Jamaican accent, "why you buggin' me? Don' you like it here?"

"Just give me a simple answer!"

"Boy, you got you'self all chewed up. Take it easy."

"T'morrow? Next day?"

"Don' know. When the doctor comes, talk to him." She shook her head and marched back to her station.

Vooko had heard enough. There were a couple expressions in the language of his new homeland that applied to the moment. *Game time. Let's kick some ass.* It took him a while, but he managed to remove the various medical contraptions monitoring his health. Then he yanked out the intravenous tubing from his arm. One phone call and fifteen minutes later, he had his clothes on and was stumbling out of the hospital and onto First Avenue. Twenty minutes later Alex was picking him up on the corner of 26th Street in a shiny maroon Toyota Camry, Pashko's pride and joy.

They drove to a storage warehouse not far from their apartment where he and Pashko had rented a small cubicle for "personal property." Vooko unlocked the door and found what he was looking for in a trunk under some DJ equipment. A Smith and Wesson .44 Magnum long- barreled revolver—a welcome gift from his cousin when he first arrived in America—and a small pile of emergency cash.

The sight of the deadly instrument triggered his memory of the day Pashko had greeted him from the driver's side of his car and motioned him to come to the window. Brandishing the freshly polished .44 Magnum, his cousin yelled out to him in English, "Welcome to America," Pashko laughed, "Look, Vooko, I'm Dirty Harry. Bang, bang."

Then his cousin solemnly gave Vooko the deadly possession, lit up a juicy spliff , and after a few hits, got sadly philosophical. "Take care with this, little cuz. This place America, ain't like home. No way. Here nobody takes responsibility for anything. They got "no fault insurance," bumper stickers and tee shirts that say "shit happens." Come on man, let's be real, shit don't just happen yo, that's what I'm talkin' about: Humpty Dumpty was pushed! Then he started rapping this rhyme about some dude calls hisself Humpty Dumpty:

Humpty Dumpty sat on a wall
Humpty Dumpty had a great fall
All the King's horses and all the King's men
Couldn't put Humpty together again.

Pashko had his groove on. He was flowin' like a motherfucker. "Now if you growed up where we did, where all kinds of devious, derelict, atrocious shit is going down, you ain't ever gonna say Humpty Dumpty fell off a wall. That's ridiculous. The first thing you gonna say is Humpty Dumpty was pushed. Right? And the next thing you gonna say is let's find out who had didded him and get that low life motherfucker for real, bro. You feel me?"

Pashko then looked off into the distance as if he were seeing the real life atrocities he had witnessed as a young man right up the street somewhere. "It's all about personal responsibility. And that's what makes us different. We know shit don't just happen, it happens for a reason." He pointed to the gun. "And that's what this here is for."

Those words rising up at him from the dead caused Vooko to flush with rage. Men, horses, ain't nobody was gonna put Humpty or Pashko together again. That was a fact. "But someone's gonna pay, old world style," Vooko vowed to the memory of his cousin. "Bet yo. I'm a see to it."

4

Scholar hated being buzzed in. It reminded him of the joint. Couldn't go anywhere without permission. But, no sooner did he mention Little Man's name than they immediately let him into the multimillion-dollar studio. It was meant to impress, and he instantly felt "bigged up."

"Hello, sir", the receptionist said. Oh, she was fine. Young thing couldn't be more than seventeen.

"You're here for the session in Studio C, right? It's around the corner to your left. If you wait here, I'll have the assistant engineer escort you."

Damn, this is just like jail, Scholar thought. *Why can't I walk my own self in?* But he said sweetly, "Thank you, young lady."

"Please take a seat. It may be a few minutes."

Scholar was happy to take a seat. In fact, he would take a whole lot more than that. He would sit and take in the oh- so-sweet smell of success. All around him hung gold and platinum albums produced in this very studio, right nearby where he was sitting.

"May I get you some coffee while you're waiting?"

"Yes, thank you. With milk…and one sugar—*if* it's not too much trouble." Scholar was putting on the charm. *This is livin', yo. I got this fine shorty waitin' on me; I'm chillin' in these leather seats, waiting for the assistant engineer to bring me into my recording session. Damn!*

"No trouble. I'll have it for you in a minute," Miss So Fine said.

Just then some white hippie motherfucker came out and messed up Scholar's reverie.

"Scholar?"

"Yes."

"I'm Kyle. Follow me."

The receptionist said, "Go ahead. I'll have someone bring in your coffee."

"Thanks." *Sweet thing.* Scholar waved at her and trailed Kyle down a long hallway lined with platinum and gold records.

The soft little white boy opened two doors, and Scholar was led into the most amazing space. In the middle was a mixing console half a block long. He'd never seen anything that impressive. It was like mad sci-fi, yo, only real. The rows of little switches, faders, and pulsing LEDs spoke to him. They said, *magic happens here.*

And there sat his cousin Biz behind the console in a big leather chair, fooling with some dials while a track blasted from these ginormous, slick-lookin' speakers. Beyond the console in the control room Scholar could see another room through the large double paned studio window. The microphone, the chairs, the wires were all in their place, clean, perfect and ordered. To his right he saw stainless steel modules mounted in racks, one on top of another; lines of small red and green diodes advanced and retreated with the dynamics of the beat of the music. This place was the bomb de bomb!

Damn. If only someone had shown care enough to introduce him when he was a young man to the possibilities that lay beyond the ghetto, where he might have seen palaces of technology like this one, where dreams could be made real. He'd have found the discipline to make it happen. Oh, what things he might have accomplished by now! It'd be legit too, yo, bet. Instead though, with no guidance or direction, he had followed the path of least resistance, ran wild, and wound up behind bars, another victim of poverty, neglect, and racial discrimination—*what a tragic waste.*

Scholar was overcome by the sadness of what might have been. But that was just for a moment, regret right now would be an indulgence that he could ill afford, a sign of weakness. It brought a brother down. So, he revved up into his jive-ass street self and said to Biz in a smirky, condescending way, "Yo, Little Man, ready to run with the big dogs?"

"We waitin' on yo' boys, yo."

"They ain't showed?"

The session was set to start at six-thirty, EST, *eastern standard time*, but Scholar had arrived exactly at six-thirty SGT, *standard ghetto time*, about ten after eight, EST. When it was confirmed that the Proof were indeed not there, he flipped open his cell and dialed. After six rings, Science picked up. Scholar laid into him.

"Chill, man," Science said, smooth as butter. They "was on the way," but they had to stop for a little "sump'm for inspiration." At nine-fifteen, EST, the Proof sauntered in with five shorties in tow.

"Yo, man, we ready to do damage," was the first thing out of Freeze's mouth. Freeze was six-three and built like a tight end. He had loose braids, no facial hair, and a diamond stud in each ear.

Scholar got up in right up face. "Where the fuck was you? Y'all s'pose to be halfway done by now."

Freeze was all up for getting into it right there, but Science, six-one, in his Nike running suit, and little wiry Pea Head, with his shaved dome and single gold tooth, held him back. Instead of coming to blows, the four blew shit back and forth until they calmed down enough for them to be able to get to work. The girls were relegated to the guests' waiting room, complete with arcade machines, a sixty-inch TV, and all kinds of junk food.

Biz wasn't sure what to expect from the hip-hop crew. Microphone technique is an acquired skill. At his best a vocalist projects his energy into the tiny diaphragm of a mic, allowing a minimum of sound to escape into the surrounding atmosphere. It is in some ways the opposite of live performance, where the object is to project sound out. With great on-mic vocalists, the resonance of the voice is mainlined from the brain to the mouth/body to the mic, and then to the recording device. In many recording sessions, singers are isolated in a sound booth, which is acoustically damped to allow only a minimum of reflected sound, the idea being that what's recorded comes direct from the singer, without ambience. As one of Biz's engineers once said to him, "A vocalist with great mic technique is able to put the essence of his spirit and make it manifest in sound."

Still, for a bunch of guys who had never been in a professional recording situation, Biz had to admit, they were doing a pretty good job. They were loose, got a flow going, and seemed comfortable behind the sheer nylon windscreens that Kyle put in front of the mikes so their *P's* didn't pop and the *S's* didn't get too sibilant. At around two in the morning, Biz got a call from Sunn.

"Yo, Biz, what you doin' workin' so late?"

"I'm working on a demo with my cousin's group. Finishing the vocals."

"Word? How's it going?"

"Why don't you listen for yourself? Here it is…"

Biz pumped the jam into the phone while The Proof listened on the super-sized control room speakers, rocking back and forth, heads bobbing, blissful, faraway looks on their faces. Scholar, contrary motherfucker that he was, had a scowl on, like his cuz was doing something wrong. After the second chorus, Biz pulled the master fader down.

He stared at the floor, phone to his ear, finger in the other one to block out the sound of everybody "runnin' they mouth" with out of control enthusiasm.

Scholar watched Biz take in what was being said. When he heard Biz say, "Word. I'll take care of it. Peace out", he got right on him:

"Yo, Little Man, who said you could play our shit on the phone? Who you playin' it for anyway?"

"That was Sunn Volt. The man can make you, cuz. I just did you a solid, yo. Now, why you getting' all up in my face?" Biz rolled his chair across the studio floor. "He liked the jam. He wants to meet wif y'all tomorrow up at his office."

Scholar reminded himself to look as if he had to think about it. But he knew who Sunn Volt was—everyone in hip-hop knew that name. He was the man, the major "playa" in the game, who had built an empire from nothing. Then Scholar, being the jive ass motherfucker that he was, did exactly what a jive-ass motherfucker who could not be straight to save his life would do: he fronted like he was doing Biz a favor by agreeing to take the meeting.

"Well, Little Man, since you already done the deed, guess we'll play your way."

Biz wanted to tell Scholar to go fuck himself, but he stuffed it; he liked living and wanted to keep on, yo.

5

From Pelham Parkway the detectives shot straight back to the 13th Precinct. As soon as Sal stopped the car Jackie bolted up to his desk with Pashko's laptop in hand. He loved unearthing the details of people's private lives, and in his experience one of the fastest ways was to mine the vast deposits of zeroes and ones on a hard drive.

The computer was an Apple. Jackie, who was unfamiliar with the operating system, took a while to navigate the folders and documents. After about an hour, though, he was able to find details of interest. What was emerging was fascinating but not quite enough to share. It wasn't until he'd been at it for another half hour that he could no longer contain himself. It was just that good. He hurdled over to his partner's desk. "Our boy was a freak, Sallie. Check it out."

Sallie squinted at the screen and saw a muscular feminine frame, nipples popping, in a scanty black one- piece suit that was cut from her chest to her navel. Under the picture, the words "Lady Panther" appeared in bold black letters. As she posed for the lascivious eye, a faux zebra-skin background waved like it was being blown by the African savannah wind. An animated silhouette of a panther stalked along the bottom of the screen. Six tabs at the left side of the screen offered more: pictures, testimonials, biography, facts, links, and contact information.

"Click on those tabs to find what you want to know, Sal. Once you've explored them, I can go through the other stuff with you."

"You kidding me, Jackie? You know I can't work these machines. Park your butt down here and take me through it."

Jackie double-clicked the tab labeled "Pictures." The site opened and six of them appeared. Under each, the viewer was invited to Click to Enlarge. They were studio- quality shots of Lady Panther in different poses, featuring various highlights of her physique.

Someone passing by Sal's desk peered over Jackie's shoulder. "Can I get printouts of those?"

"Yeah, Vince, you fuckin' perv, I'll sell you some later," Jackie said.

"Nice case," Vince laughed as he kept walking to the other side of the room.

Jackie clicked on the testimonial page. Sallie expected it to be full of oddball fantasies, gross misspellings and grammatical errors. But as he read them through, he realized how wrong he was. "These people can write, Jackie. I thought they'd be a bunch of morons."

E-mail October 11:

Before my first session with "Lady Panther" in New York in July, we talked a couple of times to get an idea of what to expect. I found her helpful and patient with a rookie. I will see her again, she really is a Lady. —Hunter in Palm Beach, Fla.

E-mail December 1:

We set right to it, and, to make it even better, she kept up great verbal work during the match. Her technique is indescribable and utterly devastating. — Beam in Laredo, Texas

E-mail April 17:

She is very strong and a very good wrestler. She is also gentle. We had a nice time. When I first met her I felt like I had known her most of my life. She is very, very pretty. —Pashko, Bronx, NY

Sal whistled again. "Well, our guy's no Shakespeare, that's for sure. What kind of idiot uses his real name on the Internet?"

"A dead one."

Sallie laughed. "Did our guy correspond with her?" He cast a sideways glance at Jackie, who still hung over his shoulder.

"Yeah, mostly about the muscle worship part of their wrestling sessions."

"Is that something I should know about?"

"I never heard of it, so I looked it up. Guys pay these ladies to pose for them in private sessions. They get off on it."

"Is there any touching or sex involved?"

"Is that wishful thinking, Sallie?"

"Definitely."

"I can look into it, if you want," Jackie flashed Sallie a grin. "Or, with all due respect, you can look into it, if you want."

Sal didn't take the bait. "So, Jackie. It looks like the vic was a freak."

"Right, and when you're dealing with freaks, freaky stuff happens."

"You and Ted interested in chasing this down?"

Jackie rubbed his chin and peered across the room. "Hey, Teddy, Sal wants to know if we want to chase this down?"

By then, Teddy had taken the laptop to his desk and was focusing intently on the website.

"Hey, Ted. I hate to break your concentration, but what about the two cars in the lot? Do you have anything for me?" Sallie asked.

Teddy didn't move his focus from the laptop screen. "The two cars in the lot?

"That's right, Ted."

Ted slowly pulled his eyes from the screen and focused them on a legal pad. "The new Audi belongs to a lawyer that works in the neighborhood. He says he spent the night with some pretty young thing he hooked up with at the club. It sounds legit. The other car is another story. It was reported stolen from up in Woodlawn two days ago. The owner is a seventy-year old retired schoolteacher. I had someone from the lab brush it for prints. We're waiting to hear."

Ted clicked on the laptop a couple of times and then read aloud: "Lady's hard-core interests are kick boxing, Jujitsu, skydiving, and dirt-bike racing. Her soft-core interests include family and friends, computer hardware and software, Internet activities, and reading about advances in medical technology and health." He finally glanced at Sal. "Lady Panther is a volunteer for the ASPCA. That's the American Society for the Prevention of Cruelty to Animals, in case you didn't know. She also donates time to the New York Animal Rescue Shelter."

Sal shrugged. "If she likes animals, big guy," Jackie joined him and in unison they said, "she's gonna love you."

The phone on Ted's desk rang. Sallie watched as his partner scribbled frantically. "The fingerprints on the car from Woodlawn belong to John Desandrio. He's an ex-con living in Brooklyn."

The leaves on the mature trees that lined the block had yet to bud, but Sal could imagine how they would provide much needed shade in the dog days of summer. The cars clinging to the curb were mostly late, mid-priced models, nothing fancy or frivolous but solid family vehicles, functional, reliable. The lawns, spotless streets and the well-kept homes could fool you into thinking you were in middle America. Closer toward the sea, Old Glory was waving in the wind, a sign to all that New York City is not a separate nation but a part of this great country of ours. As he and his boys knocked on the door of the two-family home, he was hit with a blast of cold, refreshing Atlantic Ocean air.

The mountain of muscle who opened it towered over them in the half light of the hall. But that was enough for Sal. In a nanosecond he saw all he needed to. A person could fake a lot of things, but he'd never met anyone who could fake genuine stupidity. The eyes gave it away. Sometimes, people who weren't dumb could pretend they were for a while, but no matter how hard they tried to hide it, a glimmer of intelligence would inevitably seep through. From the moment he laid eyes on the ex con, Sal knew that John Desandrio would never have to worry about that. The rock solid body of his had a rock of a brain to go with it.

The big man who slowly opened the door took in all three of his uninvited guests. "Hey, youse guys wanna come in?"

"No, Einstein, we came all the way from Manhattan to charter a boat." Sallie couldn't help himself. The detectives followed their host up a flight of stairs. Except for a set of weights, a TV on a coffee table, an old Lazyboy, and a mattress on the floor, there was no other furniture. "Mind if we take a look around?" Sallie asked.

"Make yourselves at home." The host seated himself in the one chair.

"How can I make myself at home, Johnny? You've got no furniture." Sallie gestured with a wide sweep of his arm.

"Sorry 'bout that. I just moved in."

Teddy and Jackie wandered into the equally small kitchen and bathroom, while Sallie kept the conversation going. "Do you know why we're here?"

"Can't say as I do."

"Where were you Saturday night?"

"Don't remember."

Sallie had anticipated their conversation would go like this. Nevertheless it was required foreplay. When the series of questions followed by evasive answers went back and forth, going nowhere, Sal decided he'd had enough "who's zooming who" and went straight to the sexy stuff. "We found your prints all over a stolen car."

Johnny started to rise from the chair and changed his mind. "Not possible."

"Look, Johnny boy, we're conducting a murder investigation. Just answer yes or no, otherwise I'll have you in Rikers by sundown," Sallie watched as Johnny thought it over.

"I, uh, I didn't know it was stolen. I borrowed it from a friend."

"Does this friend have a name?"

"Do I have to?" Big John squirmed.

Sallie decided to keep moving. "What was the car doing there?"

"I...left it there?"

"You left it there. Why did you leave it there?"

"Didn't want to, but when I come to pick it up, I heard shots and then I seen this guy come running onto Fifth Avenue."

"Then what happened?"

"He got hit by a car and went flying," Johnny demonstrated with his hand.

"What kind of car?"

"Black Lincoln Navigator, I think."

"Then what happened?"

"It kept going for a little then stopped. A woman come out and ran back over to see if the kid was alright."

"How do you know that?"

"Someone inside the car hollered, 'He okay?' And then she said 'He's breathin', but I think we should call an ambulance.' Then the guy said 'Do it, but not from your cell. They can trace it.'"

"Then what?" Sallie strolled to the dirty window and peered outside.

"Then the girl went to the corner box, made the call, got back in the car and they drove off."

"So now you've got this guy unconscious on the pavement and then what happens?" Sallie turned to face Johnny so he could check out his body language.

"I run in the opposite direction. All the way over to Park."

"You left the car?"

"Yeah. Didn't want to be around when the cops come." "So how'd you get home? Wait, don't tell me, you lifted one on Park."

When John was not forthcoming, Sallie gazed out of the window again. There was a late model Ford in the driveway. He nodded in its direction. "Your car out there?"

"No, sir." Johnny shifted on the chair and sat forward to lean his elbows on his knees. He stared at the floor.

"Somebody else's?" Sallie moved until he was standing directly in front of his host.

"Don't know." Johnny lifted his eyes to about Sallie's waist.

"Then you won't mind if I run a check on it?" Sallie stared at the big bozo for several seconds. "Okay, Einstein, I don't have time for this shit. I'm gonna call up your PO and tell him the problem. You guys work it out." He nodded at his partners, who were peering behind the TV and under the mattress. "Hide and seek is over, boys. Let's get out of here." As they got into the car Sal added, "And when we get back, Teddy, I want you to call Panther Lady and see what's up with this Pashko freak."

Officer Teddy Schwartz couldn't help thinking what a depraved and horny detective he was as he set up the meeting with Lady Panther at the juice bar in the high priced Equinox gym. "And bring some identity, so I know you're legit," she'd said. "You'd be surprised how many perverts there are out there."

Teddy wouldn't be surprised. Un-uh not him, because depending on what the word meant to her, he might fit the definition. Sure, he was a take-control cop in real life, but when it came to sex, he loved big women, was a fool for bondage and role-play and was unabashedly submissive. It didn't really go with his buff physique or his aggressive in- your-face personality, but, hey, his prodigiously numerous sex partners seemed to like it and he rationalized his proclivities with the progressive 'I gotta be me' attitude. And if all that made him a perv, so be it.

In her white formfitting après workout sweats that showed her "tight" body, Lady Panther did not disappoint. The e-mail descriptions were right on. Her hair was styled short and dyed the same bright red as her plump painted lips and long fingernails. Dressed for the occasion in his Mr. Muscles male equivalent tracksuit, Teddy approached her with exaggerated confidence that came from his unshakable conviction that he was one buff stud. "Hey, how you doin'?" he said, "I'm Ted Schwartz. We spoke earlier."

"Oh, the detective. Wow. I'm Shana Levy," She gave him the once-over. "Keep the shield in your pocket. I believe you. What's up?"

It took him a second to get his mind from floating in fantasyland to the immediate task at hand. "You know a guy named Pashko?" He waved at the counterman and ordered a strawberry smoothie. Nodding toward her green concoction he asked the Lady, "You want another one of those?"

She shook her head. "Yeah, I know Pashko. I love him. He's a sweetheart. How's he doin'?"

Ted was a little taken aback by her enthusiasm. "Would you mind if I ask the questions!"

"You don't have to be rude about it."

"Sorry. Let's start over," Teddy could feel the color rush from the back of his neck to his face and pressed the cold glass of his beverage against one of his hot cheeks. "How do you know him?"

"He's a client. I've seen him maybe half a dozen times. His cousin Vooko bought him his first date as a Christmas present and he was hooked."

"So you know Vooko, too?"

"Not really. I met him once."

Teddy decided to slow down to make the pleasure he was getting from the interview linger. He took a small sip of his smoothie. "What can you tell me about Pashko?"

"Hmm…Just what he told me, that he's Albanian and works at Kiki."

"Ever meet any of his friends or associates?"

"No one besides Vooko."

"Ever talk to him about…stuff?"

"Like what? Come on, Ted, what's up."

"Tell me a little more and maybe I'll let you know you why I'm so interested in him." He watched her bite her luscious lower lip. She was flirting with him.

She sipped her green thing. "Is he in trouble?"

"I promise that anything you tell me won't be used against him."

She sipped again and he watched her tumescent lips tighten over the straw then release it. "I know he was a gun nut. He used to tell me about how he loved shooting. He went to practice ranges a lot. Said if I ever needed a gun, he could get one for me."

"Did he ever say where?"

She shook her head. "Well…come to think of it, he said once that before he came to the U.S., he and his cousin had smuggled guns to the Albanian militias." Shana looked earnestly into his eyes. "Okay? I told you something. Now it's your turn."

Teddy brushed off the comment, "So what did you guys do?"

"We wrestled, over at his apartment."

"Did he ever come on to you?"

"No it was a pretty straight up thing."

"Was he tough?" Teddy smiled.

"I kicked his ass," She smiled right back.

"Do you have a list of your clients?"

"Isn't that confidential?"

"Shana, this is a criminal investigation."

"Look, Teddy is it?" Her voice was strong and confident. "I'm a professional. What goes on between me and my clients including their names is nobody else's business but mine and theirs."

"Look. It would save you a lot of trouble."

"No, it would save you a lot of trouble. And for me it would be a violation of their trust. Which I won't do, no fuckin' way."

She took her cell phone out of her bag, and started pressing numbers.

"What are you doing Shana?"

"I'm calling my lawyer. This is bullshit." Shana kept her eyes on the touch pad and didn't stop entering digits. "You told me you wanted to talk about Pashko. I've talked about Pashko. Now you gonna tell me what's goin' on?"

"Okay, I understand," Teddy said in something that sounded close to an apology.

Then, lowering his voice, "Pashko was murdered last night, Shana."

Shana clipped the phone shut. Her face contorted, she burst into tears. Black mascara ran down her flushed apple cheeks and reminded him of the pictures of China's coal-polluted rivers he saw in a *National Geographic* in his doctor's waiting room once. The expression of grief and helplessness softened her face. It was a striking contrast to her taut body and the bitch personality that he'd just had to deal with. Ted felt a hard-on coming. Shit. He needed to get a handle on his emotions. In a deliberately professional way he patted her shoulder and gave her big right arm a firm but unmistakably platonic squeeze.

"I'm sorry, here's my card." He put it down next to her drink.

She put her hands over her face, "Get the fuck out of here."

Teddy repeated in the same soft tone, "Look, I'm sorry."

"Fuck you." She walked out onto the street. Teddy followed. She waved down a cab. Teddy walked toward her. As she was getting in she looked at him and shook her head.

"What are you gonna do, arrest me?" Then she was gone.

The unfortunate big stud stood alone on Broadway wondering what his next move would be. He was a man packed for action and no place to go. In disgust he called his senior officer. He let the phone ring several times, but there was no answer.

The reason Sal didn't pick up was because it was Sunday night and Sunday nights at nine were reserved for his over-thirty-fives only, extreme basketball games at the Chelsea Piers. Sallie had been a regular going on three years. It was a total kick-ass, no-holds-barred, in-your-face- action, testosterone fest. Tough guys still trying to prove they had game.

The detective needed all the proof he could get in that department. Being abandoned consecutively by two wives had taken a massive toll on his self-esteem. The daily shock waves of anxiety that resulted took his breath away and caused his heart to kick into fight or flight mode. The irony was there was no one to fight or flee from. *They* had fled him, not the other way around.

That was until today, when his first wife, Donna, had called. It had been four years since he'd heard from the New York sophisticate with the look of the voluptuous babes in *Vogue* and the feigned modesty of *Town and Country's* too thin and too rich. Their last night together was dinner at The Odeon, too many bottles of wine, a taxi home and what he considered a mercy fuck. The next day she walked out. He should have seen it coming. Everyone else did.

And now, on his way to the hard courts, between flashbacks of their passionate last night together, he played back today's conversation word for word. First her greeting, then him recognizing her voice and being too surprised to speak, until finally, "Donna? That you?"

"Hey, Sal. Sal? Are you still there?"

"I'm here." The recognition of her voice had his heart pounding.

"From what I've heard about you, I'm glad you're still alive."

"Thanks." He was usually brilliant at asking questions, but the thought of her thick hair and coffee-colored eyes had given him a bad case of brain freeze.

"Listen, Sal, I'm sorry I called. You must be busy."

"Actually, it's good to hear your voice, Donna. How are *you*? What have you been up to since…you know?"

"I'm a cliché, Sallie. I have everything I thought I wanted, but I'm empty."

Sal was caught off guard by her candor. He waited several seconds before he said, "Okay, I'm sorry about that, Donna. I really thought that things would work out for you."

"What am I doing? I'm running the agency."

"That's what you wanted."

"I know, and sometimes when I'm flying to a client meeting or taking a limo somewhere, I feel a real sense of accomplishment. Unfortunately, it's fleeting. It's true what they say, Sal…it's lonely at the top."

"What can I say to that?"

"What about you, Sallie?"

"To be honest, I'm hanging in there, Donna. Nothing more. Stephanie and I called it quits, you know. We tried," He paused to regain his composure. "Two strikes. Nothing to be proud of, I guess. Either I'm picking the wrong women or something's wrong with me. I haven't figured it out."

"Don't beat yourself up. You're a good man, Sal."

"Kind of you to say that, Donna."

"Listen, I'm sure you're busy," which Sal had taken that to mean that *she* was and she had to end the conversation. Then she said something that made him think that maybe he was wrong. "I have a favor to ask of you, Sal. I'm coming to the city next week. One of my pro bono clients is having a reception at the Waldorf." Holding his breath, he had waited for her to continue. "If you're free, I was wondering if you would escort me."

He swallowed a huge lump in this throat before attempting to reply, "Donna, don't do this to me."

"Think about it?" she had said. "I won't ask anyone else until I hear from you. You know how to reach me."

6

Vooko took the gun into his room, chucked it under a pile of socks on the floor, and then collapsed on the bed in his street clothes. Pain seared through his entire body zapping every ounce of energy out of him. He closed his eyes and tried to forget the horror of the last few days by thinking of having sex with May, the Jamaican bartender. Damn, she was fine, and she knew how to work it, too. She always greeted him with a hug and a kiss on the cheek. And her ta-ta's. Man he loved feeling her tatas low and firm against his chest. Hell, man before he even got to squeeze them in his imagination he was in dreamland.

An hour and a half later, he woke up with a throbbing woody and knew exactly what to do with it. Nothing. All libido-depleting activities would have to take a backseat. He needed his energy for other things. He had serious business plans. By sheer will, he managed to get himself undressed, showered, shaved, and redressed. A few minutes later, he was eating a whole broiled chicken dinner at his favorite Pelham Parkway diner. Having some sustenance in his belly would give him the strength he needed to drive Pashko's Toyota down to the Kiki.

The first guy Vooko visited on his mission was Rocky Rock, a living legend to the bouncers, bartenders and doormen of New York City or, as Rocky liked to say, "the brotherhood of club security professionals." He was working the door, filling in for Vooko at Kiki.

"Vooko, you fuck. You're a hard man to kill," Rocky gave him a solid embrace. But when he let go and peered into Vooko's eyes, he backed away. "Yo, you cryin'? I meant no disrespect. I only meant love." Rocky hugged Vooko again, lifting him off his feet.

"Put me down, Rock. I know you mean good. It's all good," Vooko leaned closer and whispered, "I need to find out who killed Pashko."

"Sure you do, Vooko. I got a buddy at Speed, totally hardcore. Anything happens on the street, this guy knows. I'm gonna call him see if he knows anything."

"I appreciate it."

"Give me a second." Rocky got out his cell and dialed. "Yo, Re, it's Rock. Remember that guy Pashko I was tellin' you about? His cousin's a good friend of mine, works at the Kiki with me."

Short and sweet. Rocky dropped the phone into his pocket. "What he say Rock?"

"Vooko. Go up to Speed. Ask for Rebar. The man is a hundred-and-ten percent for real. You'll see what I'm talkin' about when you meet him."

"What's he look like? How will I know him?"

"Just get up there and ask. You'll know him when you see him. I guarantee it."

Speed, like many clubs in New York, catered to a very specific clientele. They weren't fun and gay; they weren't punk; they weren't hetero dance or Latin boogie. They were straight-up thugs and hustlers. It had started that way in the days when Wu-Tang ruled and remained the hard core's hang of choice.

The big man working the door introduced Vooko to another security guy, who was told to personally take their guest to see Rebar. They walked through a huge loft with two story high ceilings. Because it was early, the club was empty except for the cleaning crew doing their thing to some funky Latin groove Vooko had never heard before. From there, he was escorted up a staircase to another space that held a couple of long bars made of glass and neon blue lights, one at each end of the room. He was then taken up a flight of stairs. His guide knocked on a solid metal door, and when permission was received, pushed it open.

Vooko entered and his eyes swept the spacious room. It was maybe twenty feet by twenty and held enough pieces of upholstered furniture to make it seem more like a living room in someone's house than an office. A muscular man was moving casually toward him. He was a mixture of grace, beauty, and style. The clothes! His clothes alone, if they were custom and Vooko assumed they were, were worth a small fortune and that didn't include the value of the watch, bracelets and rings. Vooko relaxed. He didn't need to see much more. This Rebar was a badass motherfucker in every good sense of the word—the type Vooko aspired to become.

Rebar offered his hand, "Vooko, I am deeply sorry for your loss. We all feel for you."

For the second time, tears came to Vooko's eyes. He wanted to cry like they did in the country of his birth, but he knew it was not customary for tough guys in America to show their emotions to strangers.

Rebar patted his hand, still enclosed in his strong grip. "You know, Vooko, when one of us is killed, I take it very personally. It's a there-but-for-the-grace-of-God-go-I thing. Know what I mean?"

Vooko nodded, "I hear that."

"Make yourself comfortable, Vooko. Do you want some fresh squeezed oj?" Without waiting for an answer, he went to a refrigerator and came back with a pitcher of orange juice. Placing a glass on the end table at Vooko's right, he began to pour. "There's this crew from Far Rock. Dude running the show calls himself Scholar. They were here Saturday night getting a little loud. I wound up tossing them out around four in the morning. From what I hear, that was around the time your cousin got messed up, right?"

Vooko was surprised at how quickly Rebar had cut to the chase. He took a leisurely swig of the juice, hoping it would help sort out the mixture of feelings that were taking hold of him. "What's this guy Scholar look like?"

"Tall, wiry, light-skinned, late twenties. Got prison tats on his neck. Little tear by his eye."

"That's him."

"Watch your back, bro. His crew looked hard. I'd say all of them have done serious time."

7

Next day the Proof and Scholar went up to the label where they were escorted from the reception area past the rows of gold and platinum records into the conference room, past a stylin' blond girl. Sunn and Biz came in after a few minutes, and greetings were made all around. Nonalcoholic beverages were then offered by haughty Miss Muffy or Buffy, whatever, which the guests graciously accepted. After a few more words it was the moment of truth, listening time.

About thirty seconds into it, Sunn used his remote to turn up the volume. The bass was hard, hitting everyone in the chest with a nice full force thud. The jam was doing its thing, causing the playas from the PJ's to do some serious head bopping, a couple of them gesticulating as the music poured out and movin' lips in unison with the blaring vocal articulations. Sunn was lit up, hand on the table, bouncing it hard on the backbeat.

When it was over Sunn moved that same hand into the air and testified, "Dat's dat crack", meaning it was as far as he was concerned out of the park, ridiculous good. A euphoric spirit prevailed for a few minutes while Sun let the feeling marinate. Then he asked the group for patience. "If you have the time, I'd like to play it for my A&R man, Ray, who's just around the corner and can be over in a matter of minutes."

Scholar said it was all love, and the call was made. Ray would be right over.

While they waited, Sunn was low-key and charming, talking to the group, making them feel comfortable. He had made a point to remember their names and sprinkled them into his conversation—a practice of his, he knew how to keep the little people feeling bigged up. He tossed them softball questions like "who had made the beats? Who was doing the rap-ping?" and other stuff that they were happy to answer. When that part of the conversation seemed to be exhausted, Sunn offered that he was about to mass-market a new act called Five Star and asked Scholar and Proof Positive if they wanted to hear the about to drop "Long Prison Term."

The Rockaway crew nodded, "Sure, why not?"

The exec introduced it as an emotional ballad, the story about how "this brother was missing his girl while he was up in the joint and how he can't wait to hold her and feel her love when he gets out."

Sunn put the jam on and everybody listened respectfully. When it was over one of the Proof Positives, the one called himself Science, said he related to the song because he "had been incarcerated."

Sunn was moved by this confession and said, "Word?"

"That's right," said the brother, looking all sorry.

Sunn said, " Honestly, I feel you my brother. Too many of our people have." He was all serious and somber and shit. For a full minute the entire room was silent as if a vigil was happening or something.

Then Science squealed, "AND TUPAC WAS MY BITCH!"

The room blew up with laughter. The three members of Proof Posi-tive stood and high-fived each other like they had just won the playoffs. Scholar was smirking, all self-satisfied.

Sunn could never in his wildest dreams have seen it coming. He was momentarily paralyzed by such gravity of disrespect. Then, as if what had been done wasn't enough one of the Proof Positives said, "How's that punk-ass Five Star gonna sing about that shit when his mama still change his diapers? Who he think he is? He ain't nuttin', yo." The room had gone from chill to white hot. The punks from the Far Rock were playin' him in his own house! Things were *definitely* out of control. And that was exactly when Ray walked in.

"What's up?" Ray said. He felt the weird vibe in the room. "Am I coming at a bad time?"

Science said, "Nah, we was just playin', white boy."

Ray ignored the comment and looked over to Sunn. "What's up, Sunn?"

By then Sunn had recovered, his game face on. Revealing nothing but cordiality, he explained to Ray that Scholar and Proof Positive had something Sunn wanted him to hear. In turn, he explained to Proof Positive and Scholar that Ray was part of the decision making team at Elektrik and added that he rarely called Ray to come over on short notice, but the music was exceptional and he wanted to move on it quickly. Smiles all around.

"Okay," Ray said, "Let's hear it, then."

Sunn put it on loud and let it play through.

Ray was moved by the jam. He told the room that the rhymes were strong, the rappers had a nice flow, and elaborated that it was stone ghetto stuff—not the kind of thing that pop radio embraced, but the hard-core shit that the street felt. Sunn's associate explained that he could hear that The Proof had been weaned on Wu Tang and NWA, but they were putting their own spin on it like good artists do. Ray was highly enthusiastic, and he told the young men that, but he also added that, with all due respect, he thought some of the vocals deliveries could be improved, like maybe the group should think about redoing them.

Ray put it out there like it was no big thing, but when he finished, a death-row vibe gripped the room. All eyes moved to Scholar, who looked straight at Sunn and said, as if he were the big dog with the successful label and Sunn was the nobody, "With *all due respect*, Sunn, this shit is what it is, and ain't nobody gonna fuck with it." At that point some of the members of Proof Positive chimed in with "Word. Keep it real, Scholar."

The successful entrepreneur moved away from the table and leaned back in his chair. "Scholar, nobody gonna make you and your crew do nothing. If that is your position, I respect it. So let's you and me think about it and see what there is to see." Sunn paused for a second then in an affable gesture of hospitality added, "We're having a get-together Saturday at the Kiki. A PR thing for Five Star, come on by, there'll be drinks, food, good music. He'll be kickin' it live. Maybe once you get a taste of the show you'll change your opinion of him. Anyway, I think you'll enjoy yourselves."

And with that, Sunn got up and shook Scholar's hand, and Scholar and Proof Positive left, but not before they threw a good, long, evil, "fuck you, you don't know shit, white boy" look at Ray.

8

Sal and his detectives decided to walk over to Elektrik Records to meet the man the Captain told him had a problem that "needed to be addressed." Sal knew the Buddha well enough to appreciate the subtext of this statement: "This guy's connected; find out what he needs and get it done."

Jackie filled him in on the man by explaining that Sunn was a venerated player. Everyone knew the story. Back when Sunn was selling records out of his beater station wagon, Curtis Blow was taking hip-hop gold. The whole underground scene was blowing up, and Sunn blew up with it and never looked back. All these years later he was still having hits. His empire had gone well beyond music; he produced a television show, had a clothing line and published a magazine considered to be the last word on hip-hop. In the world of black entertainment he was the ultimate impresario.

The preamble still did not prepare Sal for the elegant man who welcomed him into his oak paneled office or for the Ivy league style of the décor. The most noticeable thing about the room were eight exquisitely framed quotations. Each one was from or about the philosopher Ludwig Wittgenstein. They were the centerpiece of a wall arrangement complemented by pictures of Miles Davis, John Lennon, Einstein, Gandhi, Martin Luther King, Louie Armstrong, Mother Theresa, and Colin Powell. From the soft leather cushion of the reupholstered Mission chair Sal studied the words of the great Austrian born philosopher.

My aim is to teach you to pass
from a piece of disguised nonsense to
something that is patent nonsense.
—Wittgenstein

Sal could see Sunn following his eyes.

"I was born and raised in New Rochelle," the entrepreneur said as he handed the men drinks. "Miles Davis had a father who was a successful dentist, both of my parents were surgeons. They sent me to Hackley Prep and from there I went to Haverford College."

Turning to Sal, he added, "Because both of my parents were born and raised dirt poor in the rural south I grew up in a household where people used African-American dialect as a first language. The way that white people spoke was always somewhat of a mystery to me. So you can imagine how difficult I found understanding the meaning behind the language patterns of my mostly white classmates. I was so consumed by language use and meaning that I became Haverford's campus expert on Wittgenstein. Hence the many quotations; they remind me of how limited a communication tool words can be."

"That's great, sir, and very interesting." Sal took a sip of water. "With all due respect, Captain Alvarez said that you had some information for us."

Sunn leaned across his desk. "One of my producers is in the hospital with stab wounds he received on Saturday night at the Kiki Club."

"What happened?"

"We had some people up at my office on Friday. He said something to them that they may have misinterpreted and found gravely—"

Sal interrupted, "What did he say?"

"He said that their demo needed more work before it was ready to be released. From their warped perspective, my associate may have come off as hugely disrespectful."

Sal sunk deeper into the comfortable chair. "Why do you say that?"

"Because they're criminals. Look, I deal in dreams, but with my artists, by and large what makes them successful is their ability to separate playing the thug for an audience and being one in real life. I'll even take it further. I got into hip-hop because I believe hip-hop musicians are the artistic descendants of blues artists carrying on a noble tradition of expression.

"One form of communication is hyperbole. Homer used it, Mark Twain did too, and so have many great raconteurs. Unfortunately, some people believe the hype. When that happens you have such incidents as I'm talking about."

Sal looked at Jackie who was nodding his head like he was in the March on Washington, listening to Dr. King delivering the "I have a dream" speech. To avoid eye contact with his smitten associate, Sal fixed his gaze on another enigmatic quotation on the wall:

> *The language game is representative of a*
> *form of life, and words have meanings*
> *only within the context of the language game.*
> —David Kramer, *Ludwig Wittgenstein*
> *and the Problem of Universals*

"Okay. So there was a misunderstanding. Your guy said something that these guys took the wrong way." Sal was beginning to feel what it was about the quotes that the Captain's friend found so valuable. He scribbled a note to himself: find out more about Wittgenstein.

"Ray's white, Detective. Which also probably has a lot of meaning to these guys. They see hip-hop as a black man's game. I think for them getting rejected by a black man is one thing, but being rejected by a white man is a sign of majority oppression in what is supposed to be a minority occupied territory. It's another example of whites having the power, and as Foucault says, "Where there is power, there is resistance."

Sal didn't have a clue who Sunn was talking about, but he knew what he was talking about. He tried to imagine what it would be like to be a poor, uneducated, black man. Despised is what he came up with, followed by loathed and feared.

"So what do you want us to do?"

"Go see Ray. Talk to him. In the meantime I'll work on getting the names of the people who I believe did this. I want them put away."

"Where is he?"

"At NYU Hospital."

"Does he have a last name? Or is he like Sting or Madonna. He just goes by Ray?"

Sunn started laughing and couldn't stop. Tears were streaking down his face. Once he composed himself he said, "Ray Lawless, detective," and started laughing again.

Sal started in too, "You're shitting me, sir."

"Detective, I shit you not, and, if I may say one more time for the record, I will get you the names of the people who hurt Ray. Expect them — soon."

If Bellevue is K-Mart, NYU is Neiman Marcus. The polished floor, security guards that act like they give a shit about security, dressed-for-success New Yorkers, and hushed ambiance say "this place is money." The three detectives were directed to a suite on the top floor, where they found a bright, sunny waiting room with a private library and home entertainment system. Sallie strolled to one of the windows and gazed beyond the East

River to Queens. If being ill was what was needed to get admission to this five star luxury house of healing, he'd get emergency appendicitis by tonight if he could...

...except for the ear splitting noise of hip-hop blasting from the patient's room. Sal motioned to his cohorts to enter. Huge baskets of flowers decorated every available space. Peering through the foliage, the detectives spotted the bed where Ray Lawless lay, head, neck and chest covered with bandages. As the detectives approached him, he struggled to locate the remote near his hand, and managed to lower the music. The movement caused him some hardship. His face contorted with pain.

"That you, Ray?" Sal asked.

"Yeah, it's me. Who wants to know?"

Sallie glanced over at Jackie. Jackie jumped in, "The po- po. Didn't they tell you we was coming?"

"Nobody said nothin'."

"Ray Lawless? That your real name?" Jackie pulled a chair closer to the bed.

"Yeah."

"All right if I use it?"

"Sure, man, just don't cash my checks," Ray gave a scratchy semblance of a laugh. "You know, they got me mummified and high as a kite, so don't hold me to what I'm sayin'."

"Where you from, homeboy?" Jackie winked at Sal. "Red Hook."

Jackie took in Ray's small pale hands. "Shit, back in the day, you must have been the last of the white Mohicans."

"You got that right. The parents overslept or was too drunk, missed the wakeup call to get the fuck out of Brooklyn before the homeboys took over."

"I hear that."

"Sunn sent you?" Ray shifted under the thin white bed blanket.

"Yep."

Jackie pointed to a big plastic bag above Ray's head, "He's the man payin' for the morphine drip?"

"Word." Ray moved his legs under the blanket.

Jackie raised his eyebrows at Sal and Teddy, who were still standing at the foot of the bed. Sal waved at him to continue with his questioning, "So what happened to you?" Jackie asked.

"Damned if I know."

"You mean you don't know what happened to you?

That's hard to believe."

Sallie gave Jackie the thumbs up and settled himself into a sofa. Ted wandered around the room examining the gift cards attached to each floral bouquet.

"One minute I'm chillin' at the bar with my man Matt, and the next minute I'm here. Just like that," Ray attempted to lift himself up but couldn't. It looked like the pain was too much.

"So where's Matt?"

"I don't know where he's at. I tried givin' him a shout, but I ain't heard nothin' back."

"So, what's Matt do?"

"He got himself a window washin' job."

"Word? Why would a big time producer like you hang with a lowly window washer?"

Ray tried to reposition the pillow behind his head. Jackie got up and did it for him. "Thanks, I owe you." When the detective sat back down Ray continued. "Oh, man, it ain't 'bout that. We been knowin' each other forever."

"So...you took Matt to this club?"

"Yeah, Matt Flynne. He didn't wanna go. Not the type. He wanted to stay home and read some book called *Guns, German Steel* or some shit like that. My man, he one a them intellectuals." Sallie had to smile; he knew the book well. It was one of his favorites, the real title being *Guns, Germs and Steel*. That didn't stop him from appreciating Ray's version though.

Jackie scratched his head and cast a sideways glance at Sal. Sal shrugged. "But Matt went to the club anyway and now you don't know where he is? That's what you're saying?"

"Yeah, man. I'm worried 'bout him. The man's a recoverin' alcoholic. Sensitive. Stuff can set the dude off and send him back to the bottle."

"So, you're telling me Matt was there when this happened to you. Would he be a witness?"

"I guess, yo. Stuff happened so fast."

Jackie sighed. "But you don't have any idea who did this to you?"

"Yo, man, no disrespect, but if I did, don't you think I'd be wanting to get them?"

"What about this group called Scholar and Proof Positive?"

"Look man. I done already told you I ain't know shit. Why don't you try to find Matty? Maybe Matty knows."

Jackie put his card on the table next to the bed "Give us a shout if you hear from him." The three detectives left the room and headed back to the station.

As the chauffeur-driven Mercedes S approached the fancy building on Central Park West and 110th Street, Sunn made a call.

"Yo, Biz. What's good?"

"Who dis?"

"Who you think this is, you lazy piece of shit?" Sunn gave it a friendly tone.

"Yo, Sunn."

"Yo, Biz. What you got goin' tonight?"

"Workin' later with the A+R boy from Warner Brothers."

"Doin' what?"

"A remix on his vanilla pop artist. Tryin' to give her street cred."

"That's cool, my brother. I'm glad the man is keepin' you busy. Hold up," Sunn shifted his phone to the other hand and ear. "Yo, Biz. Can you fit me into your busy schedule tonight?"

"I don't know, Sunn. I'm kinda jammed. Why, what's up?"

"Business. We need to talk. ASAP."

"Can't it wait 'til later, man?" he said, with a distinct lack of enthusiasm.

Sunn held his ground. "Yo, Biz. This shit ain't got time to marinate. You comin' or not, Rock Starr?" While the absence of sound came blaring at Sunn from Biz's end, he recalled a passage from Wittgenstein. During his senior year at Haverford he'd committed fragments of his work, as well as some commentary of those who studied the master, to memory. The inspired logic of the writings resonated with his passion for clarity. He had since found it helpful to refer to them, which he did often and with great effect, when situations arose that demanded extraordinary lucid thinking.

...people are trained to "react"...to the words of others.

Sunn peered out the window of his vehicle. He had the words that he needed to get Biz to "react." He just hadn't used them yet.

Biz yawned into the phone, pretending to be relaxed and disinterested, "For real, Sunn? It's a long way over to the office."

Sunn knew Biz was trying to wiggle out of the inevitable, so he did what he always did. He waited.

"Yo. Sunn. You still there?"

"Uh-huh, Biz. I ain't hanged up," He paused again. "Yo, rock star, is there a black stretch out your window by the park? Go on now. Take a look."

"What I need to look for?"

Sunn knew Biz's curiosity would get the better of him and simply waited.

"Yeah, man, I see it, a Mercedes stretch. So?"

"So, you got about twenty-nine seconds to walk your ass down and sit in it with me."

"Shit, I'll be right there, Sunn. I just got to put on some clothes and brush my teeth."

"Just get your smelly ass down here, bad breath and all. I ain't got time for foolin.' This shit can't wait."

In no time flat, Sunn saw Biz hurry through the plush lobby of the luxury high-rise and toward the big Benz. "Good to see you, Biz," he said opening the door for him.

Biz slid onto the leather seat and slammed it shut behind him. "What up?"

Sunn unlocked the leather briefcase by his side and unhurriedly lifted out an envelope; then he methodically closed it and rested the envelope on the seat next to Biz. "I got a check here made out to you for the royalties of the *Miracle* sound track that you wrote."

"That's a good thing," Biz said.

"Well, yes, it is a good thing. But, it could also *not* be a good thing."

Biz looked completely taken aback. "Not sure I know what you talkin' about, Sunn."

"Ray got cut up at my party last night. You know anything about that, Biz?"

"What you mean, Sunn?"

"That's not the right answer, Biz. But then again, it's not the wrong answer. Maybe I should be more specific. Did you see who cut Ray?"

Biz widened his eyes. "Ray was...*cut?*"

"Now think about it, Biz, because if you give me the wrong answer, this check might just lose itself for a while. It's in the neighborhood of a hundred and sixty thousand." Sunn picked it up and, after making a show of examining the envelope, he placed it on his knee nearest Biz. "If you give me the right answer you get to keep on working for me, and there'll be a lot more where this comes from. That's good. Right?" Sunn picked up the envelope again. "Now what's it gonna be?"

The limo pulled out a hundred and sixty thousand lighter while Sunn made a call to his good friend Captain Alvarez, Sal's captain, at home. After a minimum of small talk, Sunn came out with the reason for the call. "I met with three detectives today. I understand that they're investigating a murder at the Kiki last night. You may or may not know that one of my producers was seriously cut up there."

"Right. Are the crimes related?"

"I'm not paid to figure that out, Captain. I'm strictly interested in seeing that the people who did this are apprehended. "

"Me too. How can I help?"

9

Sallie took the call from the nightclub owner at his desk. "Hey, Neil, what's up."

"Sallie, I've been doing a bit of asking around and I think I've got something for you."

"You sound morose. Come on man, smell the roses."

"I can't believe you of all people just said that, Sal. Isn't that what I usually say to you?"

"Okay, talk to me."

"A week before Pashko was killed, there was a brawl at the club. It started out front and moved to the parking lot next door. Vooko got hurt pretty badly. Wound up going to the Beth Israel hospital."

"Jesus, I just saw him at Bellevue. That's some bad luck!" Sallie jotted Beth Israel on his pad.

"There was this kid that he wouldn't let into the club. He was high on something. Anyway, the kid got crazy and wailed on him."

"He must have been really flying to mess with a monster like that."

"He was. Eventually, we got him under control."

"Did you report it?"

"A patrol car came by, but by then, it was pretty much over."

"Did you get the name of the kid?"

"I didn't at the time, but I have it now."

"Who is he?"

"You're not going to believe this."

Neil sounded like he was in agony. "Come on, Neil. How bad could it be?"

"Kal Kessler. He's Sheldon Kessler's kid."

"*Shit*," Sallie could feel his stomach do a somersault.

Two minutes later, he was in the captain's office to give him the news.

"Jeeze Sallie, say it ain't so," the Buddha, as the men referred to him, leaped to his feet and then plunked down again, whirling in his chair to face the window.

"I wish."

"I've known his old man since I was a kid."

"You're kidding. Your folks had money?"

"No, neither did Sheldon's. We grew up in the same neighborhood, nothing fancy. Our folks knew each other through politics. Ban the bomb. Civil rights. Hated Nixon. Loved Kennedy." The captain turned to face Sallie and motioned for him to take a seat. "We went to what we called Commie camp together. It wasn't really Commie, but it was run by the Workman Circle, which was a progressive Jewish organization."

"I didn't know you were Jewish."

"Me? No, I'm not an M.O.T., but it didn't matter, they took all kinds, we were the original rainbow coalition." Buddha chuckled. "The camp was someplace upstate ...in Duchess County, maybe. For a city kid used to asphalt playgrounds, being up there in all that green was heaven." He put his hands behind his head and looked out the window. "Even back then, Shelly was a showoff and a bully."

Sallie leaned back in his chair and waited to hear the rest.

The captain shook his head, lowered his eyes, then peered up at Sal again, "He once beat up my little brother. It was terrible. My brother was two years younger and a lot smaller, too. It was over nothing." An amused expression brightened his face. "Man, was I pissed. When I found out, I gave him a whooping." He struck his fist into his palm. The noise startled Sal. "The counselors watched me do it too. They didn't even try to stop it. That's how much Sheldon was disliked. Can you imagine?"

Sallie only knew of Kessler from what he'd seen in the media—pictures of him confidently mugging for the camera on his boat, or, shoveling dirt at a new building ceremony, or giving a politician the instant intimacy, two- grip handshake.

"My mom's still in touch with his folks," the captain's eyes grew large with emotion. "She says Sheldon's always trying to get them out to his place in the Hamptons, but the old time lefties hate it out there. They told my mom the whole character of the place—the selfishness, the arrogance, competitiveness, the money—is something they just can't relate too. Mom gave me the impression that Sheldon's public display of his wealth is an embarrassment to them." His eyes met Sal's. "I was out there in the belly of the capitalist beast for a weekend last summer visiting my nephew. Those folks out there are something else. Scared me. The neediest are the greediest, and become the most succeediest."

"That's good, Captain. You just make that up?"

"A putz like that can be inspirational."

Sallie waited until he was sure the captain had finished his walk down memory lane, "So, what do you want me to do about the Kessler kid?"

"Talk to him. See what he has to say." Buddha wagged his finger in Sal's direction, "Be nice. The last thing I need is another fight with his old man. With Sheldon Kessler's money and his PR machine he'd kick my ass in no time flat."

Sal walked toward the door. "I'll do my best."

"Why don't I feel more reassured?"

Sallie motioned for Schwartz and Gleason to follow him to his desk. A minute into his spiel about Neil's call and the captain's orders, Teddy rocketed from his chair like he'd just won bingo, "Shit, Sallie! Remember you had me run a check on those two cars that were in the parking lot near the body? Remember I told you the fancy one was registered to a guy who gave me a girl's name as his alibi? Remember?"

Sallie nodded, but it wasn't enough for Ted. "Come on, Sal, do you really remember?"

Sal shot up too, imitating his partner's manic movements and emphatically saying, "Teddy, when I nod, I mean yes."

"Okay, sorry. He said the girl's name was Leah *Kessler*."

Jackie got up with the same manic energy, put his hands in the air and with genuine enthusiasm said, "Good work, big guy." Then gave the muscleman's hand a hearty shake and would not let go.

Teddy's response, "Okay you freak. Enough." Then with great effort he pulled his hand out of his partner's vice grip.

10

The wafer thin man on the sixteenth floor had been getting heavier and heavier into crack. And while the liabilities of his habit were becoming more and more apparent, the fun benefits were quickly diminishing. Now there was the obsessive-compulsive disorder where he was constantly checking and rechecking things. Like before he left his apartment for example, he'd unplug all the appliances to be sure everything was turned off. Electrical overloads, you see, are the cause of deadly fires and since their embryonic stages can occur behind walls, hidden, where no one can see them, great attention must be paid or lives will be lost. Thousands in fact and he'd be responsible. Crazy? No way, using the crack whack logic of his drugged addled brain Kal was just exercising caution.

Then there was the matter of his fucking keys, those elusive pieces of cut brass. They were always hiding from him, and when he couldn't find them he'd go apeshit. And he always couldn't find those stealthy bastards. So, he was in this vicious cycle in which he was constantly going apeshit. He was so messed up that he could lose and find his keys three or four times before leaving his apartment. Unfortunately, by then, he'd forget where he was supposed to be going.

And then there was the matter of his over-the-top paranoia that had combined with his obsessive/compulsive mania and resulted in a love affair with his front door peephole. Half of his time at home was spent with his eye stuck to it, lured there by the imagined stirrings of intruders or actual sounds coming from human activity in the hallway. He needed to be on guard as he explained to himself to be "on the safe side." Of what exactly was a mystery, his disturbed mind's own little secret. But watching someone while he remained unseen behind his door, was both comforting and reassuring to Kal.

Ninety nine point ninety nine out of a hundred times, the only people he ever saw beyond his door were deliverymen dropping off take-out food or the maintenance crew cleaning the halls. But his vigilance today was no waste of time. As he stood with his left eye crazy-glued to the little brass peephole, he got a full-blown look at three men walking down the corridor toward him. They stopped inches from his face. In fact they were so close that when one of them tapped on the door Kal thought the man's finger was going to go clear through his cornea to the middle of his brain. He jumped back with a little bit of a whimper, looked again and saw a shiny police badge.

Sallie could have predicted it. Kal Kessler lived in one of the obligatory renovated lofts in Tribeca, home of the many too-old-for-Williamsburg, mommy-and-daddy-will cover-the- rent poser/hipster/actor/artists. After the Ninja styled concierge gave the detectives the nod and the detectives gave her the word to keep their arrival on the downlow, they rode an elevator to the sixteenth floor. Weird, though, it was almost as if the kid had been waiting for them right at the door.

Once inside, from any vantage point, the view, the furniture, the paintings, and the enormous living room shouted "big bucks." The sun off the river was dazzling, and the light reflecting from Kal's bleached tooth enamel was brighter still.

Once Sallie's eyes had adjusted to the streaming sunshine, he examined the Armani poster boy. Kal was thin and gangly, with unusually big eyes and pouty lips. He appeared to be rather odd in other ways, too. His eyes moved from face to face much too quickly and in a disturbingly unnatural way for humans, sort of like the jerky, hyper movements of the birds and insects on the Discovery Channel. Anyone with normal street radar who'd been raised in the five boroughs could see that Neil was right: the kid was whack.

Kal strolled over to an elaborate brass and chrome coffee machine. "How about some homemade cappuccino, gentlemen? I roast the beans myself. They're the best." He said way too quickly. "I get them from a little place called Porto Rico over in the West Village." He widened his already mammoth eyes to elicit a response from the gaping detectives.

Sallie who was sitting in glaring sunlight looked past Teddy and Jackie, who were standing in the kitchen, dwarfed by an oversized Zero King. "Sounds good to me," he said. "I can tan and drink at the same time."

He studied Kal, as he ground the beans and then brewed up his caffeinated concoction. How could a scrawny bag of bones like him take down two very large and seasoned security men? The kid seemed curiously frail. "Nice place," he said, getting up from his comfy chair and strolling around the room with both Teddy and Jackie in tow.

Kal smiled. "Thank you, Detective Messina. Hey, why don't you take a seat?" He nodded at a hardwood table that looked like it could easily seat twelve.

The detectives found chairs and waited, while Kal steamed milk. Sal peered across the table to the harbor, the Verrazano Bridge, the Statue of Liberty and Jersey. The hole directly underneath Kal's window that used to be the Twin Towers was massive and the immensity of the destruction reminded Sal of how helpless he had been that horrific day. So many good people vaporized, turned to dust, gone forever, and for what? He had lost more than a dozen personal friends.

The thought of the inevitable end of existence, all existence began to envelop him as though the universe was being shrink-wrapped, and he with it. A massive wave of nausea coursed through him. For a minute, he thought he was going to lose it in front of his team members. His fingers went to his temples; he closed his eyes and massaged. "Great view. How long have you been in this place?"

"We converted the building about six years ago. It was an old warehouse."

"What do you mean by 'we'?"

"Well, I work with my father on developing downtown real estate."

"Sounds like a good business to be in."

"It has been. I hope it keeps up." Kal brought the coffee to the table on a hand-carved tray and handed each detective a red porcelain cup and saucer steaming with brew. "Now, how can I help you?" he said, seating himself at the head of the table.

"I heard you were at the Kiki Club two weeks ago," Sal said. "Did anything happen between you and some security people there?" He blew on the coffee and then put it down without tasting it.

"I was there…for maybe fifteen minutes."

"A lot can happen in fifteen minutes," Sallie waited for a while for a response, while the kid seemed to be struggling to give him one.

"Well, I went to see my sister. She was in the club with her friends. But the guy at the door wouldn't let me in."

"Why was that?" Sal lifted the cup again, this time taking a sip. He saw that Teddy and Jackie were doing the same. "Nice," he said, eying Kessler.

Sal took Kal's constipated, too tight smile as a 'thanks."

"I don't know, really. I told him I wanted to go inside to see my sister and he wouldn't let me."

"Then what happened?"

"I told him I really needed to see her. He said I'd have to wait in line."

"There was a line?"

Kal poured Teddy a second cup of the coffee. "Yes, a long line. But some people were walking right in. No waiting. No questions asked.

I asked the doorman why I couldn't, too, if *they* were going in. But he wouldn't let me in."

"Okay. Then what happened?"

"Then my sister came out and we left."

"You didn't get into an altercation of any kind?"

"Nothing of any consequence."

Kal's comment had a tranquilizing effect on the detective. It put him in familiar territory. From the depths of the ghetto disenfranchised, to the tippity-top of the money food chain, people spoke the most blatant untruths. The detective drained the last drop of the cappuccino from his cup and placed it carefully on the saucer. "We have statements from people that contradict yours, Mr. Kessler."

"Look," Kal said, polishing the table with a serviette taken from the coffee tray. "That's what happened. Some people are probably making a big deal out of something to get their fifteen minutes of fame."

Sallie scratched his left cheek. Kal's face had grown purple; he wondered if it was from repressed rage. "Have you been working in the family business long?"

"Not long. Maybe two years."

"Where's your office?"

"On Fifth and Nineteenth."

"Nice neighborhood. Did you know there was a shooting at the Kiki Saturday night?"

The kid's eyes widened again. "Really?" he said.

"Yeah. You know anything about that?" Sallie pushed the cup and saucer forward to allow room for his elbows on the table.

"No, I certainly don't."

"It was in the papers. Somebody got shot. One of the security guys."

"I'm sorry about that."

"By the way…what sort of car do you drive?"

"A 2002 Aston Martin Vanquish."

"Wow," It was Teddy sounding truly impressed.

Kal didn't respond.

But Sallie did.

He looked over at Teddy like he was going to kill him, and barked in an in-your-face Alpha-male tone. "Teddy, do you see that painting on the wall over there?" The young detective glanced at the piece of art. "That's an original Basquiat. See the one next to it? That's a Liechtenstein, and the one next to that is a Rosenquist. Take my word for it…each one of those things is worth more than we make in ten years. Compared to what he's got on the wall, the car is chump change."

The comment, which was meant to shut Teddy up didn't. Instead the muscle man came back, asserting himself with aggression in his voice, "Kessler, where were you Saturday night?" he asked.

Kal glanced at him with equal interest. "I was home with my sister and a friend."

Sal laid back. Teddy took over.

"What's your sister's name?" Teddy asked.

Kal adjusted the coffee pot on the fancy black lacquered tray. The impact of the question had initiated a series of twitches down both sides of his body. "Leah," he said. "Why do you want to know?"

"Who was the friend?"

"Our family attorney, Donny Donovan."

Ted threw a sideways look at Sal. "Does Donny own an Audi?"

Beads of perspiration were gathering on Kal's forehead just below his natural look coif. Young Armani rose from the table and carried the lacquered tray back to a position next to the fancy coffee maker. "I'm already late for an appointment, gentlemen. I will have to ask you to leave now."

Teddy remained seated. "Does Donny own an Audi?"

"I don't want to seem rude, gentlemen, but I've got to be on my way." Kal moved quickly to the front door, pushed the down button, and when the elevator came, waved the men in, then entered himself.

Before the doors had a chance to close, Kal's body jerked and he hit the wall with the flat of his palm. "Shit, shit, shit. I forgot my fucking keys." He hopped out leaving it to go down without him.

"He forgot his keys? What about his fucking head?" Sal said.

Jackie laughed. Teddy looked glum.

Back on the street, Teddy was in Sallie's face, "Hey, Sallie, what was that art lecture shit about. That was way out of line!"

"I was wrong, Teddy. I apologize."

"Fuck you, Sallie. You treat us like we're idiots. You always got to play Mr. Hotshit."

Jackie coming to Sal's defense punched Ted lightly in the arm. "Yo, big man. Sallie said he was sorry."

Sallie open handed Jackie in his arm. "Stay out of this. I can take care of it myself."

"Hey, Sallie, show him your dick," Jackie continued, unfazed by the smack he'd just taken.

"After two marriages and two divorces, I don't have one." Sallie gave Teddy a bear hug and a several quick dry humps. "Teddy, it's gone. You can't feel it, can you, 'cause there's nothing left!"

Teddy was laughing helplessly, at the same time trying to break Sallie's hold on him, but he couldn't. Finally, he stopped trying. "I give up, Sal."

Sal let go and eyed Ted sympathetically. "Are we good?"

"Yeah, Sal. We're good."

"Y'know, Ted...when I saw the moonscape where the Towers used to be, I thought of all the good men who took their last breath there. Then I looked at that spoiled, living, breathing, piece of shit in that grandiose apartment with that high priced art on the walls and it got to me. It shouldn't have, but it did." He glanced at Jackie. "We good?"

"It's all love," Jackie draped his arm around Sal's shoulder and squeezed.

"Okay, let's get something to eat and I'm buying," Sal said with child-like joy as he rubbed his hands together in anticipation of a great meal at his single favorite New York restaurant. "How about we hit Blue Smoke?"

After they parked, Sallie hustled out onto 27th Street and told the guys to go ahead, he'd catch up with them at their table. Once his partners were out of listening range he pulled out his cell phone. His hands were trembling. Christ, did he need to get a grip.

"Hey, Donna."

"Hey, Sal. What's up?"

"A bunch of stuff. You know. Things are a little crazy here."

"Sounds like nothing has changed." The response came with a major attitude.

"Come on, Donna let's make nice."

"It just came out, Sal. I'm sorry, I really am."

"Apology accepted. What's up?"

"Have you thought any more about my invitation?"

"Yeah, I've thought about it. That's why I'm calling Donna." Sal sucked in a deep breath. "I don't think I can do it. Maybe it's best to let bygones be bygones."

"Sal, if I could do that, I wouldn't be on the phone."

"What do you want me to say, Donna?"

"Say yes. Say you'll be my escort. I…I need you to do this for me." He could feel her deep humiliation. This was something new. Her groveling made him feel incredibly guilty. "Sal, please. This is really important to me. It really is."

Asking twice for something was not Donna's style. Sal could feel the weight of his depression grow lighter and then it disappeared altogether. She was begging and he was becoming elated at the thought.

"Sal?"

"Yeah?"

She must have picked up on what he was feeling. "What?" Her tone was jovial. "You shit. You're loving this. I can hear you now talking to one of your asshole cop buddies. She imitated his speaking style, "You know who just had the friggin' nerve to call me? You won't believe the balls on this woman! My first fucking ex, that's who, she was begging to see me. Begging."

Sal couldn't help it. He grinned and leaned against the car. He was eating this up.

Donna continued. "'She wanted to take me to a dinner at the Waldorf. And after all the shit she put me through. What a bitch?' Am I right, Sal?"

Sal laughed, "Right, Donna."

"So...you coming or not?"

"Can't decide."

"You can't decide. Come on Sal, I'll let you touch my titties."

"I've already touched your titties. What else?"

"These are new and much bigger titties, Sal. I had them done last year."

"Why'd you do that? They were perfect."

"I'm bullshitting you, Sal. Are you coming with me or not?"

"Okay."

"Good. You won't be disappointed. Ciao."

After homemade chips, bacon blue cheese dip, KC ribs, slaw, iced tea to wash it down and thick mud pie and several glasses of milk to cap it, they headed down to the station. On his desk a white envelope from Elektrik Records was waiting for him. Inside, he found the names and addresses of the four men Sunn believed were responsible for Ray getting sliced. The phone rang. It was the captain and he sounded like what he was, the voice of authority.

"That came from Sunn. I suggest that you run those names through the system now. From what I understand, they're all on parole. They've been fuck-ups since before Moby was a minnow."

"Captain, how does this relate to my murder investigation?"

"That's why you're a detective Sal. You get to figure these things out."

"Well how do you want me to prioritize?"

"Bring in the guys on Sunn's list first, because with his political con-nections he's got me by the throat," the captain chuckled. "The immigrant, nobody, dead guy comes in second. Really Sal, think about it, man shot dead at hip- hop club. Does anybody give a shit? Who knows, maybe we'll get lucky and they're connected. They both happened at the same place on the same night, right Sherlock?"

11

With a detailed street map of the five boroughs, Pashko's .44 Magnum, a scary-looking hunting knife, and the stash of cash he'd taken from storage, Vooko was on his way to Far Rockaway, Queens in Pashko's Toyota. The money he had with him could buy a lot of Starbucks, if they had them way the fuck out there. If they didn't, he would settle for Dunkin' Donuts'— hey it wasn't his favorite, but in his state of grief, anger, and physical pain, it was better than goat-piss mountain water, stale bread, and moldy cheese.

Coming out of the tunnel into Brooklyn, he wondered where the hood was, especially when he hit the area around the Verrazano. It all looked so quiet and suburban. Brooklyn had a rep, but based on what he was seeing from the highway he wondered why. In the Bronx, he could feel bad intentions radiating up from the streets and down from the dilapidated buildings. But what was going on here? Where were the evil motherfuckers keeping themselves? He didn't know what to make of it.

He followed the Brooklyn shore past Coney and then crossed another bridge. From high above it, he was able to make out private homes built close to the water. On his right the Manhattan skyline was in the distance. When he drove off the bridge, he headed east. The road narrowed from four to two lanes. For a couple of miles, the houses along the road had that well-kept look, the kind he would buy for his parents, when he had the money.

He kept on driving, praying for a change in the scenery. And before long he got his wish. Yes, sir! The good neighborhoods were behind him now. First, he passed by lots of crappy little bungalows. On his left, he saw the elevated train tracks. Soon, promising signs cropped up: boarded-up liquor stores, battered-looking laundromats, and fried chicken franchises, with names that most white Americans would never see in their local suburban mall.

He drove past crumbling sidewalks, several beauty parlors , one with a catchy sign called the Clip and Curl, and, finally, rows of identical apartment buildings that went on for blocks, broken only by vast parking lots for those intrepid tenants who were desperate or crazy enough to leave their cars in them. He was in the hood. And, towering above him, those massive red brick, impersonal dwellings were the PJs.

Vooko found a no-brand gas station and offered the Indian manager twenty dollars if he could leave his car there for a few hours. Ordinarily the manager would have assumed that Vooko was a cop, what else could a white guy that size in this part of the city be? But this man wasn't. Cops flashed badges and offered no money for parking. Cops didn't outfit themselves outrageously like that or have that goofy walking stride. Takes one to know one, and the recently arrived Indian attendant could tell that his visitor was an import too.

He might just as well have been wearing a sign that read, *"I am not from this country. I am from somewhere else, far away, a former Soviet satellite— a place you have never even heard of and know little or nothing about. There are thousands almost identical to me nearby in Brighton Beach and in a place called Pelham Parkway. I am doing the best I can to be a homeboy, but it ain't happening. I am in desperate need of a with-it American fashion consultant."*

"I cannot be responsible for your car," the man said as he eyed the money in Vooko's hand.

"You aren't responsible for my car. I am responsible for my car. You are just responsible for seeing that it is here when I get back."

"Okay, boss. I got your back," The manager shrugged agreeably.

As soon as the coffee-with-cream colored man said it, Vooko knew that he liked this guy. *He has got my back,* Vooko thought. *That is a good thing.* So Vooko answered his newly bonded brother with what he felt was an equally down ghettoism: "Keep it real, G. Peace out."

The gasman was impressed by the enthusiasm in those words. Surprising really, given the fear he would expect any sane Caucasian to have, who was about to venture into the surrounding streets. Instead this tall visitor gave off a barely contained expectancy, like a little kid about to enter Six Flags.

It was a warm spring night and even though it was close to eleven, people were out and about, strolling the sidewalks, playing cards, hoops, and enjoying the change from the cold weather. Vooko decided that the best thing to do was to walk around and check the place out. He put on his oversized Chanel shades and Kangol hat and faked a limp. Hopefully, the phony handicap would make him seem harmless. God help the asswipe who was actually fool enough to mess with him.

As he hobbled along the pathways that ran between buildings, alongside playgrounds, and past benches filled with smoking teenagers practicing steps to KISS-FM, he had a feeling of belonging. Here in the PJs, he was surrounded by people like himself—a minority, marginalized, disenfranchised and who, despite or because of it, had created a rich culture. It was not the Balkans, but it didn't matter. It felt like home to him, only better, because everywhere he looked, he saw multitudes of damn fine sisters. They had it goin' on in all the right places: big butts, big lips, big mouths, big ta-tas, and probably great big hearts. He took a pause for the cause, to remind himself he was on a mission.

He'd been doing the limp walk for a good forty-five minutes, when a middle-aged man in a custodian's uniform approached him. Vooko lifted his shades to read the name on the man's shirt pocket: KENTON.

"May I help you?" the man asked.

"Yo, man. I'm just chillin.' Ain't no thing."

"Are you looking for anyone in particular?"

"Your name is Kenton?"

"Yes, sir. It says so right here." The man stroked the nametag on his shirt.

"I'm looking for my homeboy Spider."

"Spider? Can't recollect no one by that name."

"Well, he's skinny and 'bout yo high." Vooko raised his hand to his chest. "He got this birfmark on his face, and blue eyes."

"He a white boy?"

"Negative. He a brotha."

"I'm afraid I can't help you."

"It's all good. I'm a find him sooner or later."

From the corner of his right eye, Vooko flashed on someone vaguely familiar. He was with three dudes, all of them together, giving off a don't-fuck-with-me vibe. They were heading toward a parking lot.

Vooko excused himself from the helpful man and limped along until he was about twenty yards behind the group. They wound up in a parking lot, standing around a brand new Range Rover. He kept out of sight and watched. They were smoking spliffs and clowning around, loose and relaxed with each other. Money changed hands and then the doors to the ride opened wide and the guys got in and sped off to wherever the fuck.

His heart was pounding so hard it was practically punching a hole in his rib cage. Vooko had found his man. No doubt. You don't forget the face of the one coming at you gun blazing, out to splatter your brains all over the pavement. As he watched the Rover's taillights fade into the distance, he wondered if he should have taken out his .44 and blown the mother-fuckers away right then and there. But all traces of doubt were removed as he recalled the wisdom of the Klingon proverb from Star Trek: The Wrath of Kahn. "Revenge is a dish that is best served cold." He had indeed, done the wise thing. Now he just had to take his time and wait for the perfect cosmic moment to beam their smelly asses up to the great beyond.

12

Black Sallie patted his holster. He liked that secure feeling and powerful surge the touch of the hard steel gave him. Eleven officers—four local, four from the Gang Unit, and Teddy, Jackie and himself—were stationed around the parking lot where they had heard Scholar and his group hung out when their day was done, anytime between three and five in the morning. Sallie's team was prepared for the worst and hoping for the best.

Around two-thirty, Sal heard from surveillance. "There's a maroon Toyota parked on the periphery of the lot. The driver is some white male with sunglasses, a Kangol hat and a pronounced limp. He gets out of the vehicle periodically to survey the area. If he weren't so conspicuous, I'd have assumed he was part of our operation, but his clothes are all wrong. He's definitely not a cop, sir. A pimp, maybe, but I doubt it. His vibe is more dick-wad than gangsta. What do you want me to do?"

"Check him out," he said.

"Roger. My partner and I are closing in on him, sir." Sallie moved until he had a clear view of the action.

From a distance he could vaguely make out the officers approach a guy with a profound limp. When they were about twenty feet away, they pointed their weapons and ordered him to move out into the light. The man was quick to oblige. He put his hands in the air. While one of the cops kept his sights on the civilian, the other officer came up from behind and removed ID from his pants pocket. After a quick glance he returned it without comment. He then motioned the man to back off and go about his business somewhere else.

"What's it all about?" Sal asked.

The officer's voice whispered back, "Some guy said he was waiting for his girlfriend, Baby Jones. The guy's a loser. We told him to beat it."

At around 3:30, Sallie watched a shiny black Range Rover pull into the lot and stop under a lone street lamp that was throwing down enough light to reveal a driver and three passengers. "The bad guys just rolled in," Sallie radioed. "Don't do anything until they exit the vehicle." As he delivered his instructions, he noticed a small foreign car racing toward the Range Rover. Before he could blink, his earphones crackled with a cacophony of warnings: *"Shots fired! Shots fired! Holy shit!"*

BOOM! An explosion rocked the parking lot before he could react. The Range Rover was immediately engulfed in flames while the swift, compact Japanese-made vehicle disappeared as quickly as it had arrived. Four dudes emerged from the heat and flames and came to a swift halt once they saw several officers with drawn guns. Hands in the air, their eyes wide with fear, with flames leaping behind them, the four young men were terrified speechless, probably for the first time in their lives.

"Goin' somewhere?" Jackie said, raising his voice to be heard above the din of the operation.

"You the guy calls himself Scholar?" Sallie said, addressing the one he quickly identified as Proof's leader.

Scholar in a panic shouted, "I'm Scholar. Don't shoot, motherfuckers! What the fuck is wrong wif you anyways?"

In all his years of trouble with the law, Scholar had never known cops to apprehend people by using firebombs. And wasn't there some kind of rule about first having to identify yourself before shooting? These officers were whack. Best do whatever the fuck they wanted before they turned him into a statistic—one more young, innocent, minding-his- own-business black man murdered by New York's Finest.

Ted and Jackie cuffed and then searched the four suspects. "The usual stuff, Sal,' Teddy said. "Some drugs, a couple of guns, and a box cutter."

"Read 'em their rights," Sal said. "Then escort these citizens to our van and take 'em in." He turned to thank the other members of their team. "I appreciate your assistance. We can take it from here."

The operation had gone well. No one had been hurt or killed. The firebomb was another story. Black Sallie wished he knew what that was all about.

The disembodied voice that the officers heard while driving the suspected perps belonged to Pea Head and went something like this. "That brother with the straight black hair and them icy blue eyes don't play, yo. He been watching too many movies. He think he Dirty Harry or some shit?" The young hood was giving the detective props for his mastery of the scene when he said, "I respect his style: shoot first, akse questions later."

Back at police headquarters Black Sallie Blue Eyes referred to a well-worn page from a book titled *Telling Lies* by Paul Ekman, the father of face reading.

In concealing, the liar withholds some information without actually saying anything untrue. In falsifying, an additional step is taken. Not only does the liar withhold true information, but he presents false information as if it were true.

After reviewing the passage, he placed the well- thumbed book back in the top drawer of his desk.

The detective could have started his interrogation of the Proof Positive members with any of the four suspects. He picked Science, however, because he liked the vibe he got off his photos as well as the name. He thought it showed a sense of humor and imagination.

"Hello, Mr. Science. My name is Messina — Officer Messina to you — and you are a guest in my place of work. Comfortable?"

"It's aw-ight, Officer Messina, sir."

"Good. Should you need anything, like a beverage or a snack of some kind, please let me know. I'm at your service." Sal pulled up a chair directly opposite his suspect. "Mr. Science—or would you prefer that I call you by your birth name? It says on this police report that it's Wardell Clark."

"Whatever, man."

Sallie used the tip of his index finger to scratch the edge of his right eye. "Have any idea why you're here?"

"Can't say I do" Science said, smirking. "Sir," he added.

"Okay, I hear you." Sallie flipped through the police report on the table in front of him, not to find things to talk about, but to convey the perception that he was in charge.

An interrogation was as much about timing as anything. His was impeccable. "So, Science, maybe this is some, er, misunderstanding?"

"Don't know, man. You the one took me in. You tell me."

"No, really. Nobody's perfect. Maybe we made a mistake. Shall I look into it?"

"Yo, man, you for real?"

"Is that an affirmative or a question?"

"Whatever."

"Well, if you don't mind, Mr. Science, I'd like to ask if you've ever heard of the Kiki Club."

"Heard of it, but can't say I been there, yo."

"Why say you've never been there? I asked if you'd *heard* of it."

"'Cause I *ain't* never been there, man. Why you doin' me like this?"

"It's just that I didn't ask if you'd *been* there. I asked if you'd *heard* of it. So I'm confused, that's all."

"Whatever."

"Well, why did you say you've never been there?" Sal leaned back in his chair and crossed his arms over his chest.

"'Cause I ain't never been there is all."

"But you *heard* of it?"

"I *said* I *heard* of it."

"But you were never there."

"Word."

Sallie leaned closer to his suspect. "Do you know anyone who has ever been there?"

Science cringed. "No. Shit, man, get outta my face."

Sallie backed off. "Let me ask you something a little less taxing, Mr. Science. Do you know any folks calling themselves Freeze, Pea Head, and Scholar?"

"Who? Don't know who you talkin' about, man."

The detective pulled five pictures from the folder and placed them on the table in front of Science. "You know who that is?" He pointed at the first picture.

"No, man, don't know."

"That's you, my friend."

"Yo, that ain't me, yo."

Sallie had already known that some permutation of "Yo, that ain't me, yo" was coming. Perp rule number one was that after every breath you took, you made something up. But he still found it funny and started laughing so hard that even Science cracked a little smile.

"That handsome guy right there sure looks like you," he said.

"Yeah, well, you know how it be. Us folks all be lookin' the same to you folks."

Sal chose to ignore this remark and pointed at the other three individual mug shots of the Proof members and Scholar, and one of them all together taken from a surveillance camera in the conference room of Elektrik Records. "Can you identify any of these gentlemen?"

Silence.

More silence.

The use of silence was one of many of Sallie's strategies. After a long pause, he gathered up the pictures and put them back into the folder. "Mr. Science, I'm going to have you escorted out of the room. I need a minute to reflect on this situation. I thank you for your time. It's been a pleasure to have made your acquaintance." He motioned for the officer in the room to escort Science to his cell.

Another officer then directed Scholar into the room and told him to sit in the chair Science had just vacated. Sal chewed on his bottom lip as he examined him through narrowed eyes. Scholar seemed angry and tightly wound and perfectly capable of everything violent that appeared on his rap sheets. He fit the description of a sociopath.

Sallie tapped the desk with the eraser end of a pencil. "Anything I can get for you before we begin?"

Scholar leaned backward on his chair lifting the front legs off the floor. "Yeah. I'll have me a coffee, light, wit' somethin' sweet. Y'all got dough-nuts?"

"We can get some. What kind would you like?"

"If you got the Krispy Kreme, dat would be fabulous, yo."

Sallie nodded at the officer in the room, who opened the door wide enough to inform someone on the other side to accommodate the perp. This Scholar was a true prince. Sal was tempted to ask if he cared for fruit slices, cheese, and liver pâté, but held back. "So, how's it going?" he said.

"Ever'thing is ever'thing."

"Everything is everything," Sallie repeated thoughtfully. "Wow. That's profound. Metaphysical. No wonder they call you Scholar." Scholar looked pleased. Sal did too. "Shall I call you Scholar, or Malik, or Mr. Johnson?"

"Scholar. Most folks call me Scholar. It's all love, man." "Love. I like that." Sal pulled the same pictures he'd

shown Science, out of the folder and placed them on the table, wasting no time. "You know these people?"

"Yeah, I know 'em. That there's me, and these is the Proof."

His candor actually surprised Sallie. It was completely unexpected. Most perps denied everything. "Why do you say these guys are proof?" "Name a the rap group, man."

"Oh. These three are *rappers*. And what are you, then? The manager?"

"You got dat right," Scholar said, cocking his head and grinning. From the satisfied expression on Scholar's face, he inferred that the man took pride in the fact. Sal referred back to the pictures in front of his "guest."

"You guys look like you're enjoying yourselves." "We was havin' a good time."

"Can you tell me the names of the people in this picture?" Sal tapped the group photo.

"Dat is Science. He the jokester. The one wit' the lid on is Freeze. He like the lover of the group. The shorties are crazy for him. And him over dere is Pea Head. He the DJ. You know, the man who roll the wheels of steel."

"So, you guys hang out together."

"You could say dat. But mostly we bidness associates." "What type of business?"

"We in the music game, yo." Scholar pointed at the group photo. "Dat was taken when we was up to our label, Elektrik Records. How you get it, anyways?"

Sallie noticed that Scholar's frown made his two eyebrows form into one long one. A quick flash of anger had moved across his taught face. The questioning was getting to him. Black Sallie recalled Ekman's passage about being better able to detect facial management, once you had gained a familiarity with the perp's facial idiosyncrasies. "I'm afraid I can't tell you that, Scholar. If I did, I could lose my job."

"Word?"

"True."

"Well, we all gots our jobs to do."

"Ain't that the truth?" Sallie rubbed the tip of his nose with the back of his index finger and then held it for a couple seconds over his pursed lips. He was getting a feel for Scholar. "Here comes your little snack." A policeman carried in a paper cup and two chocolate donuts folded in a napkin. "Hope those are okay, Scholar."

Scholar took a generous bite of the first donut. "Creamy, crunchy, fabulous, yo."

Sallie made a mental snapshot of Scholar's face at that moment. The man looked genuinely happy. His face was relaxed; his eyes radiated warmth. "So, you know the Kiki Club," he said.

As if a jolt of electricity had shot through him, Scholar jerked upright in his chair, sitting ramrod straight. Some coffee from the cup in his right hand spilled onto the table.

Sallie recalled another passage from Ekman's book: *"... when strong, the liar's fear of being caught produces just what he fears."* Scholar's reaction was a textbook case.

"Yeah, I know Kiki," Scholar said, pretending to ignore the coffee spill. "Ain't nobody in hip-hop don't know Kiki." He tried to smile, but he was too far gone. The words were right, but the tone was all wrong. He needed a time-out, like a boxer getting his ass kicked, praying for the bell to end the round. Sallie knew it and kept on coming.

"You been there recently?" "Yeah, man. Forget when."

Sallie took out a prop. "I got this list that says you were there last Saturday night."

"Don't recollect. Might a been."

"Who might have been there with you?"

"What you mean?"

"Well, the Kiki list just says 'Scholar plus three guests.'" "I'm not sure I remember specifically. May I look?" "Sure." Sallie gave him the list.

Scholar studied it. "Lots a folks at Kiki. Must be two- hundrit on dis list."

Sallie leaned forward and rested his forearms on the table. "You ever been in the joint, Scholar?"

Scholar flinched then said with an edge of hysteria, "What dat got to do wit' Kiki? I did my time. Why you on to dat now?"

Things were heating up just how Sallie liked it. He smelled blood. He loved the feeling. It made him want more. He pounced. "Do you know what a rhetorical question is?"

"Somethin' you akse someone when you already know the answer?"

"Right. You just showed me again why they call you Scholar. You've got the answers. You use big words like 'business associates.' You're smart and educated. I respect that." Sallie closed the physical space that he had purposely left open between them and leaned close enough to smell the coffee on his detainee's breath. Scholar tried to back up, but his chair was already against the wall. "See...what I'm doing is asking you rhetorical questions. I know you were at the Kiki Club. I know you were in-carcerated. I know that before you went upstate you were a juvie at Spof-ford. So, what I want to know is, why are you treating me like I'm a fool?"

Scholar smiled. He knew how to play the game, too. "Sorry, sir," he said. "No disrespect intended."

Sallie slammed his fist on the table. "Let's cut the crap, Scholar. I want you to think about this. It says on your rap sheet that you're on parole. Are you supposed to be going to nightclubs with known felons?"

"Yo. I didn't know they was felons, yo. You know what I'm sayin'?"

Sallie fixed his eyes on Scholar's. "Okay, so *now* you're telling me that you, Freeze, Science, and Pea Head *were* at the Kiki Club on the Saturday I asked you about?"

"If that's what you heard." The words were meant to be casual, but the tone telegraphed tension and frustration.

"What happened that night?"

"Nuttin' really. We was chillin' a while 'n den we lef."

Sallie narrowed his eyes and examined his suspect closely. He was lying, of course. It was written all over him. He wasn't making eye contact. He was nervously rubbing his face. "Where did you go after that?" he asked.

"Don't recollect."

"Fair enough." Black Sallie Blue Eyes turned to the attending officer. "Will you escort Scholar to more comfortable accommodations? We're through." He knew Teddy, Jackie and the Buddha were sitting in the adjacent room, observing through a one-way mirror, and got up to stick his head out the door. "It went as I expected," he said. "It's just a matter of time before he gives it up."

What the men in the observation had just witnessed was profound. In the high-stakes game of hide-and-seek that Sallie and Scholar were playing, Sallie had found Scholar out quickly and effectively. Whether Scholar knew it or not didn't matter. Sallie had exposed Scholar's inner life, then left it like an open wound to be infected by his own paranoia and self-doubt. Now it was just a matter of time before Scholar succumbed. He was a dead man walking.

Buddha looked at his watch and said, "Time flies when you're having fun, Sallie. You spent less than ten minutes with Scholar."

They all turned to watch the officer escort Freeze into the interrogation room. Teddy gave Sal a thumbs up and went to refill his coffee cup. Jackie perched on a stool next to the mirror.

Sal moved aside to let Freeze pass him and examined him from the corners of his eyes as he entered the room. The walk was aggressive, the look was a scowl of repugnance for everyone in sight. He was all edges and angles, without an ounce of fat on him. Prison gym could give an inmate the definition, but only frayed nerves and years of childhood abuse could cause someone to look so feral. "Take a seat, Freeze," Sal said, closing the door and striding to the other side of the table. "You're one scary-looking dude."

Freeze knew that. The people in his neighborhood knew that. His crew knew. Now this cop did too. Freeze rubbed his left bicep and then crossed his arms across his massive chest. "Why you say dat?"

Sal shrugged. "That's what I was feeling, so I said it. I hope you don't mind. I'm told you're a lady's man, though. Is that right?"

Freeze laughed. "Why you say it like dat?"

"I say it as I heard it." Sal waited a few seconds. "So, is it true?"

"Come on, man. What I am supposed to say? Who tolt you anyways?"

"Someone called 911. Girls were passing out all over Far Rock from being lovesick. At first, they thought LL Cool J was in the hood, but it turned out to be you." Sallie pointed at the wall mirror. "Even those guys behind the glass are nodding their heads. You've got major respect here." Sallie chewed on the inside of his left cheek. "I have to ask you some hard questions now. How you feelin'? You up for it?"

"Sure. I know the drill. You gonna play me. Try to loosen me up. Get my guard down. Whatever. It's all good."

Sallie nodded. "I'm gonna take that as a yes." He flipped through the papers in front of him. "Freeze. Were you born with that name?"

"No, man, you crazy? Name is Roland, yo. You know dat."

"I know what your name is on your police record, but I was wondering why folks call you Freeze."

"Yo. You gotta akse my boys dat. Dey been callin' me Freeze since day one."

"Can I get you a Coke or something? We fixed Scholar up with coffee and donuts."

"Who dis guy Scholar?" When Sallie didn't comment, Freeze shifted in his chair and glanced over each shoulder. "Okay, how 'bout a Coke 'n a bag a chips?"

"I'll see what we can do." Sallie nodded at the officer in the room, who went to the door and issued the order. "So, Freeze, you know these guys?" Sallie placed the picture from Elektrik in front of him.

"Nah-uh."

"How about this guy?" Black Sallie pointed to a mug shot of Freeze.

"Dat look like it may be me." "What do you mean?"

"I mean what I say—dat look like me." "Is it you?"

"Uh-uh, man, dat *ain't* me."

"How about these other guys? They look familiar to you?" Sallie showed Freeze the image taken by the security camera at Elektrik.

While Freeze was looking, the officer came in with the Coke and chips. Freeze opened the bag and downed a few. "Look, man. What you want me to say?" he asked, while still chewing.

Sallie shrugged and tapped the pictures, while watching Freeze eat the chips. "Hey," he finally said, "I've got Scholar in the other room. He identified you, Pea Head, and Science in the picture. It was taken a few days ago at Elektrik Records."

"Dat motherfucker is seriously mistaken. Whoever he is, he talkin' bullshit. I wanna see a lawyer, yo. You got no business wit' me here."

Sallie noticed that Freeze was decidedly agitated, and glanced at the officer against the back wall. He was glad to see he had his hand on his revolver. "Why do you need a lawyer all of a sudden, Freeze?"

"Yo, man. I got my rights."

An officer came in with a plastic evidence bag containing a box cutter and a second one of crack vials and placed them in front of Sallie. Sallie rearranged them so that Freeze could see the contents. "You ever see these before?"

Freeze made an exaggerated point to examine them. "Never."

"They were on you, when we picked you up a couple hours ago."

"Someone must a put 'em on me. I ain't never seen 'em, man."

Sallie sighed and handed the containers back to the officer. "I have a feeling you're not being a hundred percent truthful with me, Freeze. I have a feeling that if we check the fingerprints on the box cutter, they might be yours. I have a feeling there might be a little blood there, too."

"Suit yo self, man."

"Scholar said you were at the Kiki Club the night a guy was messed up with a box cutter. That's attempted murder. And the drugs? Man, forget it. With your history, you could be gone a long time."

"Scholar don't know shit."

"I thought you didn't know Scholar." "Fuck you, man."

Sallie reinserted the photographs into the folder. "You want another Coke?"

"Yeah, I could use another one."

The mood in the interrogation room had shifted. Whereas before, Freeze had been angry and defiant, now he had grown pensive. Sallie had seen this dynamic many times before. Freeze was changing strategy. The stabbing thing was bad, given his record, and he knew it, but being in possession of all that crack, given his priors, was the nail in the coffin. If he didn't cut a deal with the DA, he was looking at serious time. The lead detective came back at him, "So, you were saying, about Scholar—"

"Dat punk better not be talkin' no shit 'bout me. Punk motherfucker."

Sallie sipped at the iced tea in front of him and waited a little then asked, "Why is that?"

"Man, I got shit on him dat'll put his punk ass away from here to eternity. Look, man, I wanna see a lawyer. I ain't playin.'"

"I'll get you an attorney, if you tell me what you know about Scholar."

"Yeah, right."

"I give you my word."

"Un-uh, I ain't playin' like dat."

Sallie waited and watched. Freeze ate chips and sipped Coke and squirmed on his hard chair. He kept one eye on the officer, whose hand rested on his holstered gun. Sallie waited a full minute longer. Finally he said, "Would you help this gentleman secure legal representation?"

It was just then that the captain walked in accompanied by the lawyer and civil rights activist Kenyon Parks. Without preamble the captain said, "You got to let them go, Sal."

13

Sallie shouted at Ted from his desk across the expansive room, "I want to talk to that attorney Donovan."

"I already tried his office," Ted said. "He didn't come in today. I got his cell and his home numbers. I've been trying them, but he isn't picking up."

"Where does he live?" "Up in Mamaroneck."

Sallie shoved several folders to the right corner of his desk and reached for his suit jacket. "Let's take a ride. I could use a little country air."

"Can't we leave it until tomorrow, Sal? I'll keep trying his phone."

"Can't wait. We've gotta do it now, Teddy. Something's way off base here." Sallie had his jacket on and was hovering over Teddy's desk. "I want to get to the bottom of this Kessler connection. First we've got the whacko son trying to hook up with his sister at the Kiki causing all kinds of hell to break loose. Then you tell us the Audi in the lot the night of the Pashko murder belongs to Donovan, who said he was with a young woman that night, and that woman turns out to be Leah Kessler. Then Kal Kessler tells us his sister, Leah, and Donovan were with *him* that evening. We need answers. Was Leah Donovan's young thing? Is he more than her father's attorney and friend? There's a lot of weird coincidences concerning this family. Something's fucked up here."

Westchester County is located just north of the Bronx, about a half hour from downtown Manhattan, without traffic. It has one of the highest concentrations of wealth in the world. The average house is priced around $700,000. Donovan's place was worth at least ten times that. The white colonial was situated directly on the Long Island Sound where the competition for water views made property values sky high. The rolling lawn leading down to the water, the pool, tennis court and seven-car garage added up to mega bucks, even by the incredibly priggish local standards.

From the outside, everything was immaculate. It was one of those places where the pebbles in the driveway don't dare stray onto the lawn and every single blade of grass remains closely connected to more of the same. An apartheid really, pebble and grass, separated by a cemented, cobblestone border. That was until Jackie picked up a pebble and tossed it onto the lawn.

"Why the fuck did you do that?" Ted asked. "It was just something I needed to do, Ted."

"What...the separation of grass and gravel was bothering you?"

"No, Teddy. It's more the idea that I have the power to add a little disorder to Donovan's perfectly ordered world."

"You think you just did that...by throwing a pebble onto his lawn?"

"Maybe not, Ted, but it made me feel good."

"Then I guess you showed *him*, Jackie." Ted threw a sideways glance at Sal, the three of them acting like kids at a playground.

Sal laughed, "Leave it alone. We've got more important things to do." Sal grabbed hold of the substantial doorknocker and it thumped loudly as it struck the massive oak door. He deliberately wanted to make a major "don't fuck with me" racket. Donovan was a hot shit lawyer and this was a wake-up call. If the guy was taking an afternoon siesta, naptime was over. No one came. "Take a quick look around the property, Jackie. We'll wait here."

Sallie banged on the door again. "Mr. Donovan, it's the police. Please open the door."

Jackie returned while Sallie was still banging away on the door. "He's got a cigarette boat hanging above the water by a lift, four cars in the garage, this guy knows how to live. I feel like I'm in Miami Vice minus the flamingoes and palm trees. No sign of him, though. Still no answer here?" Sallie shook his head. "Let's pop the door and see what's going on in here. Muscle man, do the honors." Teddy took off his jacket and got poised to do some damage. "Be gentle," Jackie said. "That's one beautiful door.

Looks hand-carved."

"We're gonna open it, not fuck it, Jack. Besides, I thought you wanted to rock this guy's orderly world." Teddy took a too handed grip of the solid brass door handle, twisted it and gave the door a shove. To his surprise the unlocked door swung open without force, "What the fuck?" Teddy said as he peered through the doorway into the front hall.

"What the fuck what, Schwartz?"

"The fuckin' place is completely trashed. That's what the fuck."

Sal pushed Teddy out of his way. "Holy shit! Someone's been on a rampage." In a defensive crouch with his weapon drawn, Sallie crept through the hallway and into the living room with Schwartz and Gleason following closely behind him. The sofas had been slashed to ribbons, the lamps were in pieces, a plasma TV screen had been eviscerated and left on the dining room table with the carving knife still in it, and the dining room chairs had all been overturned. The kitchen was a disaster, as well. All of the food in the cabinets and refrigerator had been tossed onto the granite countertops, in the sink, and onto the Saltillo tiled floor. Crystal glassware and china were piled in shattered pieces next to a wall left pockmarked from the force of their impact.

Jackie whistled. "Looks like someone had a problem with the hors d'oeuvres."

"Funny goes a long way on this job. That's why I like having you around, Gleason," Sal said. "What do you think, Schwartz?"

"Funny. The guy's funny."

"Let's go upstairs and see how they liked the main course."

Sal cautiously led them up an imposing marble and oak spiral stair-case. Three quarters of the way to the top landing, they found Donny. He was propped up against a banister with a bullet hole in his chest. As they got even closer, they could see Donny Donovan was dead. Sal who always conversed with corpses as if they might talk back, directed his words at the deceased lawyer, "You must be the chef."

"Hey, Sallie. You want some tea? I just steeped a little peppermint. Goes good with these banana muffins." The captain reached for one, and started to peel the paper from its sides.

"No, thanks." Sal slouched on the chair and steeled himself for the lecture he knew was coming.

"You know who called me this morning?" "No, sorry sir, I don't."

"Care to give it an educated guess, Sherlock?"

"No, sir, I don't." Sal replied, attempting to get up from his chair. "Please don't prolong my agony. Just kill me and get it over with."

The captain was unmoved. "Stay seated, Sal. I decide who dies, and when and how they do." His eyes bored holes into the detective's. "Sunn called. He was wondering when we're going to get those punks off the street."

"Soon, sir."

"That's not good enough." "Okay, when then?"

"Sunn says there's this Matty who witnessed the assault on his friend Ray. I want you to find him ASAP. We'll get a statement and take another shot at those masterminds."

"What about Kenyon Parks? Won't he just get them out again?"

"Sunn says no." "How come."

"Sunn told the man The Kenyon Parks Scholarship Foundation would receive a large infusion of cash if he stayed away."

The captain pointed his finger at Sal. "There's an aspect here that I think you're missing."

"What is that sir?"

"You're dealing with an Albanian dead man. Albanian, Sal. You been to Arthur Avenue recently? All those old Italian places are now owned by Albanians."

"With all due respect sir, you're being obtuse."

"Right, I am. I was hoping you could connect the dots." He picked up his teacup. "They didn't get there by making nice. They're tough. The dead kid worked security for Neil. Maybe he was working security for some of his countrymen, too. Maybe his friends are not taking kindly to the fact that someone took out their own."

Sal let out an audible sigh and looked at the ground. "Okay enough about that. Tell me more about Shelly

Kessler's kid."

"Ted and Jackie are in Far Rockaway as we speak. We just found out Kal works there and that's where the perps are from. We're looking for a connect."

"Shit."

"It's sad, really. The son's a user. Looks like he hasn't slept in months— shaky hands, runny nose, red eyes—you know the deal. I think the sister might have similar issues." The Buddha looked at him with a combination of approval and pity. "I'm sorry to hear that," he said, finally, both appearing and sounding truly sympathetic. "Nothing's worse than having fucked up kids."

"The Kessler kid claims that on the night of the shooting at Kiki he was at his lawyer's, Donny Donovan. But, Donny's car was in the lot the night of the murder."

The captain nodded. "Go on."

"On Sunday, after we ran the plates we called Donny. He told Ted he was with his girlfriend by the name of Leah Kessler. Of course, then it meant nothing to us. But on Monday, Neil Weinstein says Kal Kessler was at the club a week before the murder."

"The kid must have made an impression."

"Yes, he did, as a matter of fact, both he and his sister did. Turns out Kal and Leah were involved in a violent altercation with the doorman, Vooko, who happens to be Pashko's cousin. Then, last Saturday night, Vooko was critically injured in a hit and run, and his cousin Pashko was murdered. Both of the incidents happened in close proximity to the Kiki."

"It's getting interesting."

"So, we have two Kessler kids mixed up in this. Leah connected to Donny whose car was at the murder scene, and Kal who had been involved in an altercation with Pashko's cousin the week before. Yesterday we tried contacting Donovan to get his version of the story."

"Which is?"

"We never found out. We couldn't get a hold of him so the three of us went on a little fishing expedition to his house in Westchester."

"Lawyers, fuckin land sharks. You find him?"

"Not so funny, captain. We found a dead land shark." It was hard to surprise the Buddha, but Sallie had just succeeded.

"How?"

"Shot. Mamaroneck police are doing the ballistics, now, as we speak."

"So how does this tie in with the murder investigation?" The captain narrowed his eyes and twiddled his pencil. "Are you saying one of Kessler's kids killed this Pashko?"

"I'm not sure. Like I said, Kal told us that he was at Donny's when Pashko was killed. Donny's dead, so we don't know what Donny would have said."

"So you gonna talk to Leah?" "That's what I was going to do next."

The Buddha took a sip from his steaming mug. "What about the Far Rockaway crew that has Sunn so concerned?

Can you connect them to the killing?"

"Not yet, but they were at the club that night."

"This Donny Donovan thing is likely to get a lot of media play," the captain scrubbed his face with his hands and then rubbed his eyes, "More shit to contend with."

Sallie nodded. "You're probably right. When we went through his house, we found pictures of him and the Kessler family all over the place. I got the impression Donny and Sheldon were close buddies. Some of the pictures were taken on golf courses and tennis courts. Looked like they spent a lot of time together."

"What's Donovan's story?"

"From what I gather, he was sort of a local boy made good, the father was a fireman, mother a nurse. They still live in a small two-family in Mamaroneck. Nothing fancy. Donny was a tennis star, went to Harvard and then to NYU Law, with a specialty in real estate. Started out working for one of the big uptown firms, and then opened his own place downtown. I think Sheldon set him up."

"What'd he look like?" "The son of King Kong."

"Did you go to Harvard, Sallie?"

"You trying to undermine my self-esteem?" Sallie knew his mentor was busting his balls. "I went to John Jay, same as you did."

"Just keeping you humble, Sal," the captain grinned. "Big guy, huh?"

"Around six-three, two-forty." "Gay?"

"Nope. Not good looking enough."

"Funny." Buddha didn't even crack a smile. He rose and stretched his long arms over his head. Sallie marveled at how much the large gut resembled the statues of his namesake. "Stay with it, Sal. I'll keep the wolves at bay. And Sal," the captain gave him a hard look, "Get me more info on the Molotov. My money's on the Albanians on that one."

14

"You fucking slut," Kal uttered sincerely and with great pain. "You couldn't keep your hands off of him, could you?" When it came to his sister, Kal didn't miss a thing; she was his dream girl and family savior, but now she'd let him down.

"You're just jealous, you little shit." She cradled the cell phone to one ear as she distractedly brushed her hair.

"Come on, Leah help me out here," Kal pleaded, "You know dad hates my guts."

"You blame him?" "Leah," Kal whined.

"Why are you being such a little dick?" she paused. "Someone's pounding on the fucking door. I gotta go. Bye, Kal."

"Police, open up." Sallie lifted his hand to knock a second time. He heard some movement behind it. The occupant was checking him out through the peephole. "Open the door, please," he said.

A female voice replied, "Let me see your badge."

Sallie raised his shield to the peephole. He hated whiny female voices.

"Okay, just hang on a minute, will you." More whine. The door swung open. "May I help you with something?" The young woman didn't move from the entrance.

Sallie pocketed his shield. Ebony hair, green eyes, petite, she was gorgeous. "Leah Kessler? I have a few questions and then I'll be on my way. Won't take up too much of your time."

Leah hesitated long enough to give him a quick scan, then stepped back and waved him inside. She looked wasted. "It's a good thing, because I don't have much time to give you," she said, holding her head higher than necessary. "I suppose I don't have much of a choice. Have a seat."

She gestured toward the massive living room couches that faced the Statue of Liberty and points beyond. The apartment was of the same luxury line layout as her brother's, only two floors up.

Dirty dishes were piled up in the sink and overflowing onto the granite counter top. The garbage looked like it hadn't been taken out for months. Ditto, the dining room. The expansive marble table was hidden under piles of clothes, tossed about randomly. He pulled his eyes back to Leah's face, her make up perfect, hair shiny clean.

"Sorry about the mess," she mumbled, reading the disgusted look on his face. "My girl hasn't been up here for a couple of days. Would you like some Diet Coke? I'm afraid that's all I have to offer you. I wasn't expecting company this morning."

"A Diet Coke would be great, if you don't mind."

While she was in the kitchen, Sal ran his fingers over the dust-covered furniture. He noticed the ashtray filled with cigarette butts and half-finished spliffs.

"I can't seem to find a clean glass," Leah said, poking her head into the room from the kitchen doorway. "They must all be in the dishwasher and I haven't run it yet."

"Forget the glass. I'll take it right out of the can," Sal said, while wandering around the room.

He removed a pen from his shirt pocket and poked around the ashtray, finally leaning over to smell the contents. Then he marched to the wall of windows and peered out at the same depressing view of the gaping crater that he'd taken in from her brother's place.

Leah returned with his soda then plopped onto one corner of the couch and pulled a pillow over her abdomen, sighing audibly from the exertion of having to play hostess.

"Your eyes are like, sky blue, detective. Yours or contacts?"

"Mine since birth," he said. "Do you know where you were the Saturday night before last, Miss Kessler?"

"Hmm...I'll have to think about that. One day seems to float into the next these days. Let's see . . . I get my nails done every Thursday afternoon and have my hair done on Friday mornings. Other than that, I'm running from one event to the other. I have trouble remembering what happens when these days. I'm always on the go." She shook her head and shrugged. "You know...I really can't remember what I did a week ago Saturday night."

"Have you ever been to the Kiki?" Sallie stretched, then covered his mouth to hide a yawn.

"The Kiki? That's the club off Fifth, right? I've been there a couple times, I think."

"Were you there a week ago Saturday night?"

"Can you give me just a minute?" Leah closed her eyes and then peered up at the ceiling. "Yeah...I might have been there." She threw a quick glance at her inquisitor.

Sallie emptied half the can and put it down by the ashtray. "Remember who was with you?"

"That's asking a lot, you know? It seems like it was years ago." She frowned, and with great effort said, "I think I was there with Donny. Yeah. It was Donny Donovan."

"I assume you mean Donovan the attorney." Sallie meandered to the couch and sat on the edge of the coffee table, leaning forward to rest his elbows on his knees. He was within two feet of the wide-eyed young woman. "Anyone else?"

Leah pulled her legs up under her and clasped her arms around the pillow, as though they might protect her from him and his questions. "Kal came for a little while. Then we left."

"You left with your brother Kal?" "Yeah. I think I did."

"What about Donny?"

"He stayed a while longer and then he went to his office to do some work. His office is real close to that club."

"So...did you see Donny after that?"

Leah shut her eyes again and massaged the pillow. "Yeah, I think that was the night I picked him up and we went up to his house."

"Where's that?" "Westchester. Mamaroneck." "Was your brother there, too?"

"I don't remember. It's a big house."

"Your brother claims he was with you and a friend at *his* place that night."

Leah's eyes widened and darted around the room. "He did? Look. I don't remember. I said I had trouble remembering things like that, didn't I? We're all out somewhere almost every night. We have a lot of friends."

When he noticed a few tears shimmering in her eyes, Sal softened his voice. "When was the last time you saw Donny?"

"You mean like...the most recent time? You...you have me all confused now."

"You didn't see him last night by any chance, did you?" "Last night? You just asked me that, didn't you? Listen, can't you see you're upsetting me? I'm . . . I'm not used to being spoken to like this." She wiped her eyes with a corner of the pillow.

"Leah, would you just answer the question? Did you see Donny last night?"

"No. No, I didn't. *I didn't* see Donny last night." She threw the pillow onto the floor and rose from the couch with her hands on her hips. "What's all this about, detective? Why are you asking me all these questions about my...my attorney?"

"I just came from his place." "So?"

"Donny Donovan is dead." Sal thought the alliteration added a light touch.

Leah definitely didn't. "Oh, my fucking god!" She leaped from the couch and headed for the door, whirling to face her interrogator. "You're shitting me, right?"

15

As usual, the Battery Tunnel was backed up, and the fumes from the commuter buses in front of them were making the two detectives a little punchy. "You know, Teddy, I wish that Kessler kid wasn't so full of shit," Jackie said.

"Which one?"

"Probably both, but right now I'm talking about the tweaker."

"Which one?"

"You think they're both tweaking?" Jackie threw Teddy a sideways glance.

"Unless that fucked-up way they have of going about things is somehow genetic."

"I'm talking about Crackhead Kal." Jackie reached over to turn up the air conditioning.

"By definition, if you're a tweaker, you're full of shit, Jackie. That goes without saying. Lying's just how they do. The facts speak for themselves."

Jackie cleaned the foggy window next to him with his forearm. "Kal Kessler doesn't develop upscale Manhattan real estate with his dad, like he said he did. Instead, he's a 'managing supervisor' for the Kessler Group, which runs low rent housing for the city of New York. Why couldn't the little tweaker have told us that in the first place? I wouldn't have thought any less of him." The last sentence was loaded with sarcasm.

Teddy made a left-hand turn and swerved to keep from hitting a speeding yellow cab.

"Exactly. That's my point. As a tweaker, it's in his nature. He's not able to be forthright. He lives to fuck things up. Listen, Jackie, you know the joke on the street? What's the difference between a junkie and a tweaker?" Teddy glanced over at Jackie expectantly.

Jackie grinned. "The junkie will steal your shit and bounce; the tweaker will steal your shit and then say he's gonna help you look for it." He laughed even harder than Teddy who had tears rolling down his cheeks.

Twenty minutes later, they arrived at the Frederick Douglass Houses. The buildings were clean and free of graffiti. Newly paved blacktop connected several playgrounds, filled with kids playing while young moms watched them. Older residents socialized on the benches. "It's a beautiful day in the neighborhood," Teddy sang, as he synchronized his stride with Jackie's.

"I hear that. Somebody here is taking care of business." Jackie said, gesturing at the grounds.

The management offices were located on the ground floor of a large building in the center of the complex. A cheery receptionist greeted the detectives.

"Is Kal Kessler here?" Jackie asked.

"I am sorry to say that he is not," the woman said. She was poised and dignified, mid-sixties. She reminded him of his aunt on his mother's side.

"Do you know when he'll be in?" Teddy asked. The woman rolled her eyes. "I wish I did."

Teddy scowled. "We were under the impression he has an office here." He pulled out his badge.

"He does, but Mr. Kessler, he does not keep regular hours."

"I see."

Teddy shrugged at Jackie. "What should we do?"

Jackie turned to the woman and said in his most charming way. "Is he ever here, ma'am?"

She perked up. "Yes, sir. He's here sometimes."

"Well," said Jackie, "that's a start, isn't it?" He gave her a big friendly smile. "Ma'am, is there anyone on the premises that he works with... someone we could talk to for a few minutes?"

"There's Kenton. He's in charge of maintenance. Would you like to see him?"

"Yes, please." Jackie turned toward Ted and mouthed, "I love this woman."

"Just one minute, please," she said. She reached for a walkie-talkie on her desktop. Once she was about to speak, her demeanor changed. No more Miss Peaches and Cream. No sir, she was all business. "Kenton," she said sternly. "Get on up here, man. Do not be takin' your sweet time, neither. The police is here and they want to talk to you."

Teddy knew it was Kenton as soon as the tall, well- groomed middle aged man arrived. Kenton greeted them affably with a confident look in the eye and a firm handshake.

"Why don't you gentleman use the conference room?" The receptionist pointed at the door to her immediate left. "No one's gonna bother you in there. The coffee pot is perkin' and the soda machine is full." She waved at Kenton like she'd shoo away a fly. "You know where it is. Go on now. Show these officers the way."

When the detectives were seated in the semi- comfortable institutional chairs next to a perfectly matched and scratched wooden table, Kenton went over to the soda machines. "You gentlemen want something to drink?" he asked.

"I'll take a Diet Coke, please, and the Hulk here probably wants some bottled water. Am I right?"

Teddy nodded.

Kenton inserted the quarters.

Teddy removed the notebook that always occupied the inside pocket of his jacket and a pen from his shirt pocket. "You work with Kal Kessler?" he asked, eager to see where the interrogation would take them.

Kenton took a deep breath and let out a sigh. *"Shiiiiiit."*

"It's like that, huh?" Jackie asked.

"Oh, yeah, it's like that and then some." Kenton handed the detectives their drinks and took a seat.

"Is he your boss?" Teddy opened the bottle and took a swig of the water.

"Technically speaking he is." "When is he here?"

"Well, he comes around here every once in a while." "How much is every once in a while?"

Kenton rubbed his face and deliberated. "Well, let's say maybe once or twice a week."

Jackie leaned forward, while creating wet circles on the tabletop with the perspiring Coke can. "What's he do when he isn't here, Kenton?"

"That's a good question." Kenton let it hang. "Does he associate with anyone here?"

"Well, I heard from one of the cleaners that he spent some time up in apartment 10C, Building 5." Kenton smiled.

"Who lives up there?" Jackie emptied the Coke can and crushed it.

"A college girl and her cousin. It's their parents' place, but they're down South. These days, the girls have it all to themselves."

"What was he doin' up there? Kessler."

"Maybe you should ask them. They're usually in about now."

Jackie cracked a grin. "Ain't nothin' happenin' 'round here you ain't know about, huh?"

Kenton grinned back. "I take care a business. You know what I'm sayin'?"

Teddy pocketed his notebook and rose from the table. "You think you could take us over there?"

Kenton pushed back his chair. "Sure thing. Be my pleasure."

Within a few minutes, the three of them were in a floor- to-ceiling, wall-to-wall, clean, earth-toned Sear's-decorated living room. Tatiana, a full-bodied, glossy-lipped, young African-American woman, dressed in a drastically modified Harvard T-shirt, ushered Teddy and Jackie to the couch.

They took a seat. Jackie immediately began studying a large painting on the wall opposite them. It wasn't at all like the confusing, modern crap Jackie remembered seeing on Kal Kessler's living room walls. This was much better. Real. The scene was of a mill on a running stream, putting him in a peaceful state of mind, and the deer painted in the foreground walking through meadows of high grass, that was a beautiful animal. Behind everything was a golden sunset. Man what he would give to be there now with his big Savage model 110. That there Papa of Bambi'd be venison stew in no time flat.

Meanwhile Ted had begun to work on Tatiana, in a seductive Barry White basso profundo. "You know Kal Kessler, ma'am?" he asked, once again removing his notebook.

"I can't say I know him, but I've met him." Tatiana glanced from the floor to Ted's face and then quickly down at the floor again.

Ted grinned. If she was in college, he was ready to enroll. "Where you meet him at?"

Meet him at? Jackie thought. *Damn, the sublime shorty got him going so that he be ending his sentences with prepositions.*

"You know Darius?" Tatiana asked.

"No, I don't. Who's Darius?" Teddy threw Jackie another sideways look to let him know that the moment of High Alert was now.

"He work for Kenton." Tatiana scowled at Kenton, "Why you not tell them?"

Kenton was cool. "I left that for you, baby girl." "Whatever." She waved her perfectly formed hand and

then flicked her elongated finger at him, indicating that at the moment he was of no significance.

Teddy noticed that her painted nail extensions had palm trees on them. She was the total shit. "What's he do, Tatiana?" he asked.

"He cleans and whatnot."

"So...what does he have to do with Kal?" Jackie leaned forward, to make sure he wasn't going to miss what was coming.

"That's a long story."

"We've got time, young lady." Jackie said.

Tatiana adjusted her T-shirt and placed her hands on her hips to emphasis the curves of her ample breasts. "Well... one night Darius akse me do I want to meet someone. I say who he got in mind? He say a friend of his, some rich, white boy with a nice car. I say okay with me. He say he can come by with his friend and is my cousin Aisha around, 'cause Darius, he kinda like her."

Teddy listened intently to her voice, while trying not to get an eyeful of her magnificent everything else. She was driving him crazy and she knew it. So did Kenton and Jackie. So would anybody that could see.

Ted adjusted his tie. Tatiana strutted in front of him. "So we all up here and, you know, the four of us, sittin' and talkin'. That white boy, he wearin' this fine suit and I say to him where he get it at. And he tell me somethin' like Bergdorf's, which I ain't never heard of. Then he akse me 'bout myself. I tell him 'bout how I be takin' night classes at Queens College."

"We heard." Teddy made a big deal like he was impressed.

"Yeah?"

"What are you studying?"

"I'm a be a physical therapist. My friend Ginnel, she one. She doin' good, real good." "Then what happened?"

"We had us something to drink. Got relaxed. You know."

"So like you two had a little thing goin' on?"

"I think he pretty cute, you know, for a white boy." Tatiana glanced at Jackie, to see his reaction. "They can be cute too, ya know." He was unmoved. "Then Darius say somethin' like 'ain't she fine?' Then I put on some music and we start dancin' slow-like." Tatiana swayed her hips to Teddy rubbed his forehead. She was playing them for all she was worth, and he was feeling her in a major way.

"Then we was getting' a little romantical and such. I had lit a few candles. Then that boy Kal, out of nowheres, he tell me he not feelin' too good. He got to leave to get him some fresh air."

"Then what?"

"He left and Darius, he follow him." "Just like that."

"Word. They was gone."

"Wow." He wouldn't have gone. No way. He would have stayed for the whole show and stuck around for the rerun. Teddy wrote a few things in his notebook.

Tatiana pouted. "It hurt my feelings like. But later on, Darius, he come back and he tolt me the boy got issues."

"What kind of issues?" Tatiana looked at Jackie.

"Girl," he said, "this here is a homicide investigation.

Whatever you got to say, you better say it now."

"If you put it like that." She hesitated. "Well, he tolt Darius he didn't think I was his type."

Teddy rose from the couch and sauntered around the room, sweeping every nook and cranny with his eyes. "What do you think he meant, Tatiana?"

"He go for them girls out on the street. You know, raspberries, crack whores...nasty girls. Am I making myself clear?" Tatiana looked as though she had just drunk a mouthful of sour milk. "Getting' 'em two at a time. Like that." She looked at Jackie, who looked at Tatiana and then at Teddy. Another sign, a small acknowledgement that Jackie knew that his partner was a little nasty, too. Ted stared right back at him and nodded. Confirmed, he was a dog.

Jackie faced the woman, who was now preening at Kenton. "You still tight with Darius?" he asked.

"We friends." "Where is he now?"

"He probably workin'. Why you not akse Kenton?"

The detectives turned in unison to Kenton, who was examining the floor while shaking his head. "I think we best be going," he mumbled.

Outside now and on their way to his office, Kenton got Darius on the Motorola and told him to get over to his place. A couple of minutes later a friendly-looking, neatly dressed young man stood in the doorway. Kenton introduced him to the detectives, "Gentlemen, this here is Darius."

Teddy flashed the badge and didn't waste time with chitchat. "You know Kal Kessler?" he asked.

"Yeah, I know Kal. He's the managing agent." "You guys hang out?"

"Not really. He's my boss."

Teddy motioned to Jackie to take over in his own inimitable way. Jackie came to his side and glared at the young man. "That's not what we heard, playa. We heard you is tight."

Darius frowned. "Where you heard that?"

"Look, man, this here ain't a social call. We on business.

So don't be fuckin' with us."

The change from casual to straight up was immediate. Darius definitely had gotten the wakeup call, "Ya know, I knew this was gonna happen. I had even talked about it with my uncle Javon. He a supervisor at the home depot by the Brooklyn Bridge."

"Oh yeah. What did your uncle say?"

"He say, ain't nothing good gonna come from you hanging out with no rich white boy."

"Well he a supervisor for a reason, young man. He knows the way the world works, hear?" Jackie looked at the name written on the shirt. "Darius, what do you know about Kal Kessler?"

"Look, we hung a little bit. No biggie." "Yo, Darius, I'm keepin' it real with you." "Where this goin'?"

"Little brother, *this* ain't how it go." Jackie acted agitated, like he was about to throw a punch, deck the dude. Instead he opened his fist and poked the young man in his chest with a finger, while he spoke to him. "We the po-po. You ain't. We akse the questions, you answer the questions. Now I'm not gonna akse again."

"I forget the question." Darius scratched his head and screwed up his face like he was about to cry. "You fuckin' my head up, yo."

"You do some smoke with that white boy?"

"A little bit, yo, but mostly I ain't about that. Know what I'm sayin'?"

"Look. I know he doin' somethin.' We seen him yesterday. Man was jumpin' outta his skin. Who he hang out with when he come here?"

"I don't know nothin' bout it. I keep myself to myself." "What about Tatiana?"

"That there was a one-time deal, yo. What else can I say?"

"You know anyone 'round here name a Scholar?"

From the periphery of his vision, Teddy saw a worried look appear on Kenton's face. He came in fast. "Kenton, let's bring you back into this discussion. I'm asking a simple question. Work with me. Have you ever met a guy named Scholar?"

Kenton swallowed and glanced at the three men whose eyes were riveted on his. Reluctant to reply, he finally said, "I've seen him around, but I don't, like, know him know him."

"Ever seen him with your boss Kal?"

Once again, Kenton seemed to be reaching deep, searching for the correct answer. "I don't recollect so."

Teddy continued. "I think you're not being a hundred percent honest, Kenton, and, right now, ninety-nine per cent isn't working for me."

"Why do you say that?"

"I don't know. I just got a feeling about it."

"Well, it's the truth. I'm not lyin'." Now Kenton looked like he was the one about to cry.

"This ain't goin nowhere, if you ain't gonna come clean, yo." Jackie jumped into the conversation, aiming his contribution at Darius again. His voice was a combination of urgency and compassion. "Nobody gonna know, boy. This here is like how they say about Vegas, 'What's said here, stays here.' "

When neither of them spoke up, Jackie stood closer to Darius. Too close. "I swear, yo, we ain't fuckin' around, little brotha," he said. "I mean it, what's said here stays here."

Ted draped his arm around Kenton's shoulder and squeezed. "Same message applies to you, Kenton."

"Word?" Kenton said. "Word."

With great reluctance Kenton said, "Okay, man. Kal and Scholar hang."

Teddy threw Jackie a glance that suggested huge satisfaction, then looked at Kenton, who was staring at Darius. "I'm not taking the hit, boy," Kenton said. "You want to keep your job, you tell them what they want to know."

Darius shifted from one foot to the other and jammed his hands into his jeans pockets. "It's on me, yo. I introduced 'em."

"Let's hear it," Jackie said.

"One day, me and Kal was in the boiler room smokin' some shit. Fucked us up good. He say it so good, it make him want to suck his own dick." Darius looked around like he was waiting for a laugh. When none came, he shrugged and continued, "He akse me where I get it from. I say 'tomorrow I'm a hook you up wit the man that solt it to me.' Next day, I did. The rest is all love."

Jackie intensified his gaze on Darius's face. "So, those two be hangin' out a whole lot?"

"Word. I hear they be doin' all kinds a shit together." "Oh, yeah? Like what?"

"I heard they been clubbin' in the city and hangin' in the Hamptons."

"How you know about the Hamptons?"

"Man, that shit is all over the place. You seen Vibe last month? Russell Simmons be out there, and Diddy. It's the joint."

Jackie faced Ted with a pumpkin grin. Ted grinned back. The irony of some kid in the heart of one of the city's poorest and most crime ridden neighborhoods knowing all about the wealthy domain of New York's power elite was not lost on him, and no way lost on Jackie. Being African-American himself, he probably felt a certain amount of pride. Some of his people had broken the barrier and made it out into the promised land of milk, honey and a whole lot of money.

"Thanks, little brotha, you did good," Jackie said, patting Darius on his shoulder. Then he turned to Ted for a high- five. "Looks like my people be movin' on up, bro. Movin' on up." He grinned again, shaking his head and showing his big pearly whites.

16

Vooko lay back in his bed, stoking a nice blunt. To keep from becoming completely overwhelmed over his cousin's sorry-ass death, he thought back to the bright pulsing light that beamed from his rearview mirror as he sped away from the burning Range Rover. Gasoline orange and yellow, like a campfire, only flashier. He hadn't planned on throwing a Molotov cocktail. It was all about that American idiom—necessity is the mother of invention. He knew the expression but something about doing it made the words come alive.

Last night, by some beautiful chance of fate, he had found a discarded piece of garden house near his front tire. He used it to siphon gas from his tank into an old Smirnoff bottle Pashko had left in the back seat. He'd taken a rag from the trunk and stuffed it into the bottle. That was his fuse. Satisfied with his handiwork, he parked his little car out of sight and waited until the big Range Rover returned to the lot. Throwing the thing while driving was tricky, so was getting the shots off, but what a way to end the hunt. Blazing! It was pure bad-ass, next-level motherfucker shit. Pashko would have been proud of him.

But the memory of the blast was not enough to take the edge off of Vooko's rage. In his dark mood, his thoughts drifted to high school social studies, of all places. From there, he reviewed what he remembered about the American legal system and the idiotic presumption of innocence. The first time he'd heard of it, he couldn't believe his ears. *Maybe,* he'd thought, *I am misunderstanding the meaning of the words.* When he realized that he hadn't, he had started giggling uncontrollably in the middle of Social Studies class. His teacher asked him what he found so funny. For the first time all that year, he spoke up in her class. "Evils exists," the words came with the pain of his long repressed pathos and suffering. "I have seen it. I have seen innocent people murdered for no reason. It is crazy what went on there. My cousins were raped and we could not help them, my neighbors were shot in front of their families as we stood waiting to be killed next. This is the truth." The class fell silent. What could they have said, the innocent Americans.

After his short diatribe, he had admitted to himself with profound clarity that, given the right circumstances, he would have been evil, too. Rape Serbian virgins? Sign me up. Butcher their mothers and fathers? Why the fuck not! He knew lots of folks who had. They considered themselves normal. Went about their daily lives as if all was well. He imagined they blamed their unspeakable acts of violence not on themselves but the exceptional circumstances of their times.

While the THC in his lungs cruised to his grey matter, he found he wasn't getting high, he was getting low. His next mental pitstop; humans were guilty, conniving, low- life motherfuckers, and, as far as he was concerned, any system that bestowed the benefit of innocence increased the potential for evil to triumph. (Bestowed? Where the fuck did that word come from?) His rage amped up and he zoomed into overdrive with thoughts about stupid, naïve Americans, when would they learn that if it looks like a duck, walks like a duck, and quacks like a duck, it's a duck? Shoot it and eat it for dinner. If the duck had a gun, he'd do the same to you in no time flat.

Jeeze, what kind of shit was he smoking? Was it dusted or something? He felt all lonely…way lonely and sad and depressed, like he was teetering on the edge of a the big scary thing he had seen on The Discovery Channel that the narrator proclaimed, sucked up matter and fucked with time or bent it or some shit. Oh yeah, they called it a black hole. Damn, he was starting to wish he were dead. That was something new. What the fuck was that about? He needed to get up and head out, do something that would make him feel better. He had business to take care of.

Vooko forced himself to shower, shave, and put on some fresh clothes. In his Nike sweats and his neo-classic Adidas, he left his apartment and started to walk to the diner of international cuisine. Today he was feeling a Greek omelet, French fries and some spicy hot American buffalo wings.

After he'd entered the diner, he decided it would be less lonely at the counter, so he chose a stool facing the street. The extra distraction would do him good, keep the bad thoughts from messing with him. The old-timer sitting next to him got up to leave and asked Vooko if he'd care to take a look at his paper. Moved by the considerate gesture, Vooko nodded, "Why, yes. Thank you."

The Russian waitress took his order. Since his arrival he had changed his mind about what he wanted. "I'll have a root beer and the burger de-luxe with home fries well done."

Usually, he didn't like girls from that part of the world, because they seemed slutty, the way they dressed and strutted their stuff...and mad greedy. But this one was more quiet and serious. Maybe she was working her way through college. Maybe, he thought, when he was feeling more like himself he'd ask her out, go to City Island for dinner.

While he waited for his meal, he thumbed through the paper. He found pleasure in touching the thickness of the pages. They were firm, but soft, too. Someone must have put a lot of time and effort into coming up with that kind of quality. The print was nice, too, so black and neat. It was easy to believe a story that was printed with ink on paper like that. Usually, he turned to the sports pages first, because that was where the automobile ads were located. Looking at those beautifully constructed machines, at prices he could almost afford, made all things seem possible. Today was Wednesday, not much to see, so he moved to the front of the paper pretty quickly.

The first few pages didn't hold his interest. They were filled with international bullshit and celebrity crap. But when he got to page five, he saw a picture of a guy he'd seen at the club. What a rush, actually seeing a familiar face in the paper. It said his name was Donny Donovan and he was found shot to death in his waterside home in Mamaroneck. Vooko remembered him...a big guy like that, all decked out in money gear, was hard not to. He remembered thinking the man was a celebrity, the way he strolled over to Bobby, who sent him straight inside. Later, he asked Bobby about him and Bobby told him Donovan was "a big money lawyer" who had an office around the corner not far from the Kiki. Bobby's connect with Donovan was that they both drove Audi A8's, which they parked in the lot next to the club.

Right next to the photo of Donovan was a picture of his house. A monster crib! Then there was another one of him on a big ass yacht. In that picture, he had his arm around an older guy. Vooko pulled the paper closer to his face. Another dude in the background looked like someone familiar, too. *Holy shit! It's the ass-wipe that messed up him and Bobby at the Kiki that Saturday night.* Vooko shifted his focus back to the two older men. They looked like Big Willies mugging for the camera, each with a cigar in one hand and holding up a good-sized fish with the other. Had they been in Florida or on one of the islands in the Caribbean? The kid in the background looked like a third wheel in the party. Under the picture, it read: Donovan and New York real estate tycoon Sheldon Kessler (foreground) and Kal Kessler (background). According to the writer of the article, nobody knew who had killed the attorney, Donovan, and the police were pursuing different leads.

Vooko chugged down half a glass of water. He'd bet big bucks Bobby was totally bummed—first Pashko and now his Audi buddy and both killings within forty-eight hours. He felt a little sorry for Donovan's friend,

Sheldon. Like him and Pashko, they were forever separated. Everywhere, the world was a dangerous place. Whether you had enough green to chill on a yacht or you were just a fuckin' immigrant trying to get by...everything turned to mud.

Vooko moved on to the next page. Once again, he was stunned by what appeared in front of him. In all his years of reading the paper, he had never seen anything about anyone he knew. What was going on? Staring him in the face was a picture of four seriously bad-ass thugs. One of them was the one who had shot Pashko and the three others were his friends who had been in the car when Vooko torched the motherfucker. *Whoa!* Right next to it was a picture of the burnt-out Range Rover. He was fuckin' famous, but with Pashko gone, there was no one to tell.

The story was about how this dude—Professor Kenyon Parks, a high profile local politician wannabe—was able to get the young men released from jail, because the police had used excessive force—incendiary devices and unprovoked shooting—when taking them into custody. The paper made it sound like those PJ motherfuckers were civil rights heroes! What was up with that?

The young assistant sound engineer, who'd been up for twenty-hour straight hours and had at least another sixteen to go, handed Biz Harrison the phone without screening the call. The producer took it from him without thinking. He should have known better.

"Yo, Little Man."

Biz thought he must be trippin'. Were his ears working right? The voice on the phone sounded like his cousin Scholar. How could that be? "That you, Scholar? I heard you got busted. You callin' from the joint?" This last part being more like wishful thinking.

"Man, we busted outta the joint. Ain't you read the paper?"

Biz felt his stomach move into his mouth, like when the elevator went up too fast. He had to chill. His life depended on it. "What's up, rock star?"

"Hey, man, I ain't the rock star. You is."

Scholar sounded downright friendly, which made Biz all the more suspicious. "Okay, Dogg, I feel you."

"What we gonna do with our joint?"

"I don't know, yo." Biz swallowed again. Sweat beads were forming on his forehead. He thought he'd never be hearing from his cuz again. Damn. The call was like the end of that movie *Carrie*, when the girl's hand came up from the grave and started choking somebody. Man, he practically had wetted his pants.

"Seein' as we in the papers 'n all, I figure you could maybe help us see some movers and shakers." His voice had that familiar edge to it. Scholar was on a mission.

Biz tried to ignore his request. He changed the subject. "You in the papers? What for you in the papers?"

"Check out the *News*, Little Man. We be in there wif Professor Parks. We blowin' up. It's bananas."

Biz could not believe what he was hearing. "Hold on, cuz. I'm sending someone to get it." He put his cuz on hold, and asked the assistant engineer to fetch him the paper from the receptionist. In an instant, he was paging through it. When he had located the picture and write-up, he got back on the line. "I see it."

"Course you sees it, Little Man. So what you say 'bout it?"

"It's all good," Biz said.

"Come on, man. Hit me wit some connections."

Biz wiped the free running sweat from his brow. The last thing he wanted to do was introduce his psycho cousin to the other label execs he knew, especially after that disaster meeting with Sunn and Ray. His brain was cranking, trying to think of an exit strategy. "Yo, cuz. I'm tied up today."

"You da man, blood. Don't be doin' me like dat."

Biz wondered why everything Scholar said had an implicit threat. "Why you don't call 'em, now that you famous 'n all?" he said.

"Little Man…you trippin' on me."

Biz felt pure panic coming in. "Look, man," he said. "I told you I'd produce one joint, which I did. I ain't agree to nothin' else, Scholar."

"'I ain't agree to nothin' else, Scholar,'" Scholar mimicked, in a high bitch-tone whine. "You got my money, Little Man. And I got me a joint that your boy Ray say is sub- standard, need more work. You ain't did what you was s'posed to of done, accordin' to our agreement."

The walls of the studio were closing in on him. The little man heard ringing in his ears. His heart was doing double time. "Okay, okay, Scholar. I'll get back to you." He hung up quickly and noticed that his hands were trembling. The situation with his cuz was seriously fucked up. He dialed Elektrik Records. "Sunn Volt, please. Tell him Biz is calling."

As he waited for the big man to get on the line, he had a feeling of emotional disconnectedness, as if everything that was happening to him was happening to someone else. He needed some serious deep breaths to calm himself down, to get his soul back into his body. The assistant engineer shoved a note in front of him, written on Post-It pop-up paper. "There's someone in the lounge. Says he's your cousin."

Biz stared helplessly at the young man who had just written the message, then at his engineer, who was waiting bleary eyed for instructions for what to do next. The designed-to-be-dead-quiet control room was fast becoming a fertile breeding ground for his jumping nerves. Every second that passed seemed to intensify the physical discomfort his anxiety was causing him. His head ached. He felt nauseous. There wasn't enough air in the room. He was hyperventilating.

Then he heard a familiar voice in his ear. "Yo, Biz, Sunn here. You see the newspaper yet?"

They were lovin' it. Thanks to the lawyer Brother Kenyon Parks the four unfortunate victims of the trigger-happy NYPD were once again free men. Better even, The Proof were local heroes, symbols of the struggle. No justice, no peace and shit. With pictures in the paper, faces on the tele, they was famous, yo! To celebrate their freedom from their illicitly obtained incarceration they had celebrated with much exuberance, illegal substance indulgence, and fornication. But that was yesterday, and right now it was time to take care of business and there they were kickin' it in the artist's lounge, spread out on the leather furniture, tv tuned to BET, while their manager was inside the studio with their producer discussing what was in store for the future.

"Thank the lord for Brother Parks," crowed Pea Head. "That man saved our asses, man. The police department is out of control." Science flopped himself on the velour couch.

"Motherfuckers is whack! I need to relax." Freeze took a large toke on a big stick then passed it to Science lazing in a comfy chair on his right.

"There's no doubt about it," Pea Head said admiring his plush surroundings. "We started small yo. We was nothin', but look at us now. A nasty-ass bunch of next-level gangsters 'bout to blow up America." Referring to himself, he said, "Give some props to the genius who recognized early on that all the negative, fucked-up, criminal things we did out on the street had the positive effect of giving us cred and local fame."

"Word up, Pea. It was you. Respect, yo," Science said. "And we hyped it to death," Freeze said explaining what happened next. "I swear man I was putting our shit out there, biggin' us up 24-7. Every chance I got, I bigged us up, made us legends, talked about like who we had robbed, the dealers we beat on. Come on gentlemen, how 'bout some props for the man that had got the name Proof Positive spread all over the street like a sewer backup?"

"Yea, yeah, I'm feelin' dat." Pea testified as he and Science performed an abrupt collision of hands from their prone positions.

"Yo, you think we gonna hear from Sunn?"

"I cain't predict what a motherfucker gonna do. Damn, Sci, you think I'm a side kick or somethin'?"

"Man, ain't he loved our shit?" Pea Head threw out.

Science squeezed out a little encouragement. "Ain't nobody bust it out like us, yo. Fuck Sunn. He just one a many."

"Yeah," Freeze said getting indignant. "From what I hear, he cheap, too. You know Rodney over in the East Tower? He *tolt* me dat Rashid signed to Def Jam for a quarter mil 'cause Elektrik wouldn't come up with the green."

Freeze slammed his fist into a pillow. "Word? Rodney tolt you dat? He some cheap ass motherfucker."

"Not only dat, man," Pea Head said, wanting more of the limelight, "but Rodney say someone he know say Elektrik can't get no money outta da label to do a video."

"What's dat to us, yo! We gangsters. We too thugged out for TV anyways! Dat's what I'm talkin' about."

"I hear dat, too," Science said. For good measure, he added, "Truth is, when I heard dat weak Five Star joint over at Sunn's, I had me some serious doubts if I even wanna to be on the same artist roster as his punk ass."

Sal got lucky and caught a cab the second he hit the street. Traffic was light, and he was out on Park Avenue under the brightly lit entrance in ten minutes. Meeting Donna under the best of circumstances made him jittery, but this was worse. His tuxedo, that had once hung loosely on his muscular frame, now had a vice grip on his balls and was straight-jacketing his chest. Being squeezed and restricted, he felt any minute he'd wet his pants, stop breathing, or both.

"Sal, over here!"

"Donna, you look gorgeous." Which she did. Age had softened her. She was more voluptuous, womanly.

Donna smiled. "You're all red, Sal. Are you okay? No, you're not. I can see you're completely out of breath. Do you need to sit down?" She steered him into the lobby of the hotel and then led him to a plush chair. "Sit here and I'll go get some water."

Sal breathed a sigh of relief. Time alone was exactly what he needed. As soon as she was out of sight, he unbuttoned his tux and took in a long, deep breath, blowing it out through pursed lips. Within seconds, Donna was back.

"Here, Sal, drink this."

The water was bottled of course, and cold. He took a few swallows. "Thanks, Donna. I'm a little overweight." He had meant to say over*worked*.

"Me, too," she said. "The extra weight looks good on you, though. I always thought you were a little thin. Now you look macho, Sal, *very* macho, I like it."

"What's that saying about flattery getting you somewhere? You're gonna give me a heart attack." Sal took her hand and gave it a tight squeeze, "It's good to see you, Donna. You haven't changed a bit. You're beautiful."

The ballroom was glittery and gold. The cocktail hour had ended and the room was nearly full of seated guests who were already picking at their salads. The detective looked around the room taking it all in. This was the top- of-the-food-chain Manhattan that Sinatra sang about in *New York, New York*. No little town blues for them, these folks could make it anywhere. Extreme living. Their New York meant swimming in a tank of piranhas and loving it. They wouldn't have it any other way. He recognized a few politicians, two A-list actors, and a couple of Donna's old pals from work, but he didn't see anybody from the job or Chelsea Piers.

Donna seated herself next to an elegant woman with lots of jewelry, clean skin, and big, straight teeth named Connie Goldberg. Sal thought she could have been forty, except her hands said she was older by at least two decades. She had vitality and was sexy and self-assured and she knew it. Throughout the evening she would jokingly introduce him to the guests as her latest and final husband, to which Donna would say, "No, he's not, Connie. I brought him here and I'm leaving with him."

Sal was flattered by the female attention. It made him feel good, like maybe he had something special going on in his life. When the band slowed the tempo down to a bump and grind, Donna raised an eyebrow. "Okay, Sal. It's time to pay for your dinner. Are you ready to get on the floor?"

Sal would have swept the floor, if she'd asked. He was intoxicated by her, the wine, the setting, and the music. "Anything you'd like, lady," he said, helping her from her chair.

They danced. Her arms wound tightly around his neck, and her lush scent cascaded over him. She pushed her hips against his, and as one of his felons would say, he "practically busted a nut." One slow dance led to another. He was in a state of high arousal and delirious submission. *If someone could shoot me now,* he thought, *I would die a happy man.*

As the slow jam went on, his mind took a detour to darker places—the places where suspicion and paranoia lurk, where great detectives have an open ticket, easy access and where nothing happens by chance. It is the world where the truth, in ever morphing disguises, hides in plain sight.

Sal shifted his gaze from the other dancing couples to Donna. Her eyes did not meet his. He followed their direction. There were a lot of people she could have been looking at as that part of the room was packed with sequins and tuxedoes. But, Sal kept looking for the answer to an unformed question in his mind when he spotted the real reason why he was on the dance floor with her. The missing link, the most logical reason he was there and why he was destined to remain in his personal heart of darkness.

"Would you mind if we sat now?" he asked. "I'm ready for dessert." They returned to their table, and as he ate the rich chocolate soufflé, he wondered how he should proceed. Should he pretend that he couldn't have predicted what would happen next? Should he leave before the introduction was made? Maybe he shouldn't assume anything. Maybe he should believe the reason he was here had more to do with Donna and nothing to do with the man in the crowd. But, the likelihood of that was too overwhelming. If he were a gambler, he would have to bet that tonight was going to be one more disaster in the long line of disasters that defined his love life.

Connie rose from her chair. She had her back to Sal, but he knew what was coming next. He listened while she spoke to the gentleman who had just arrived at their table. "My dinner partner this evening is the very charming Salvatore Messina. Have the two of you met Sheldon?"

Sal rose to greet the man. Connie beamed. "Mr. Messina, this is my good friend Sheldon Kessler. He is quite a celebrity in our city. Perhaps you have seen his handsome visage in the newspapers."

"How are you both? Nice to meet you." Kessler extended his hand. Sal shook it and then introduced his date for the evening. Kessler acted as if he and Donna were strangers, but at the introduction, Donna's face turned crimson.

"A pleasure," Sal said. Donna nodded.

"I've read about you, Mr. Messina. You've done some very courageous police work."

"Thank you, Mr. Kessler."

Connie touched his sleeve with her freshly manicured hand. "I had no idea you were one of our city's finest, Mr. Messina. What have you done to elicit such praise from Sheldon?"

Kessler answered for him. "He's well known for his undercover work, but he was in the news for saving a hostage during a robbery in Soho last year. It was in all the papers. Front page of The Post, wasn't it, officer?"

"Kind of you to remember and doubly kind of you to say, Mr. Kessler."

"Don't be so modest, detective." Kessler's smile was one of condescending arrogance.

Sal nodded politely and waited.

Connie was still in her gushing mode. "I saw your name in the program, Sheldon. Are you active in the Education for All project?"

"Only as a contributor. I like to support any organization dedicated to improving the educational pursuits of those who need a helping hand. The mayor is a strong leader in encouraging private initiatives. I'll do anything for a friend." There it was, the message of the evening delivered as subtly as a shovel in the face. Kessler was telling Sal that he knew about the investigation, that he was a buddy with the mayor and, of course, that he knew a thing or two about Sal. And now Sal knew a little more about Donna. It was an edifying moment all around.

"How are you, detective?" The familiar voice came from out of nowhere. Sal turned to see a beautifully serene couple. "This is my wife Cheryl."

Sal shook the hand offered him. "It's a pleasure to meet you, Mrs. Volt. Isn't this a coincidence?"

Sunn smiled. "And I see you've met Sheldon Kessler and Connie Goldberg." Sheldon got a healthy handshake, Connie a kiss.

"This is Donna Ciccone," Sal said, "the woman who was kind enough to invite me tonight."

More handshakes.

"Congratulations on the turnout, Sunn." Connie turned toward Donna and Sal. "We call Sunn and Cheryl 'Mr. And Mrs. Anonymous' in our literature. Their contributions are behind a great deal of our funding."

"Congratulations," Kessler said.

After a few more niceties, Sal and Donna were alone at their table. "Thanks for coming, Sal. It meant a lot to me."

"Thanks for inviting me, Donna."

"Do you want to come over to the hotel for a drink?"

"I'd like that, Donna, but I can't. It's been quite an emotional night for me. If you don't mind, I'll put you in a cab and head home."

"You're sure that's what you want to do?"

Sal shrugged and watched the remaining guests as they headed for the entrance to the banquet hall. He felt depressed. The night had gone so wrong. "Yep. That's what I want to do," he said. He pulled out Donna's chair and steered her toward the exit. Outside, he put her in a taxi and took the one right behind it. "Follow that cab in front of us," he told the driver.

The radio blasted West African music, while the heater blew unwanted warm air. They were heading north on Park. Sal could see Donna's silhouette in the lead cab. She was resting her head against the back of the seat. "Could you turn the music down and the heater off?" he asked.

"You want the heater off, sir?" "Yes, please, and the music down."

The pounding syncopated rhythm ceased. The hot air kept pouring out of the ducts.

"What about the heat back here?" Sal was getting even more irritated.

"Sir, I have this problem. I cannot turn it off."

The dispirited detective opened the window and placed his face where the cold night air could find it. Anything was better than that constricted feeling with the heat blowing on him and the images of the night's debacle fast forwarding through his overactive mind. At Fifty-ninth Street, they made a left and kept going to Columbus Circle, where Donna got out. Sal waited until she started to walk west, then followed her on foot to one of the new hotels in the Time Warner complex. In the enormous high ceilinged lobby, he felt even smaller than the evening had made him feel. He wanted to shout at the top of his lungs, "Somebody step on me. Finish the job."

Donna took the elevator to the forty-third floor—the China Bar. Sal waited a full three minutes and then, filled with self-loathing for what he was doing, grabbed an elevator to floor forty-three.

The panorama when the doors opened was movie-set spectacular, glamorous people twittering, silhouetted in a backdrop of the brilliant night lights of the city. He found a place on the balcony behind a column, where he thought he could watch without being observed.

"May I get you a drink, sir?"

He jumped. It was the waitress. What did he expect? He was in a bar. "A Coke. Regular. Not diet." With an attempt at casualness, he glanced over each shoulder to inspect the tables near the windows. He didn't see Donna, but he saw Sheldon at the far side of the room. He seemed to be looking for someone. Sallie continued his surveillance, hoping he wouldn't see her, but now that he did, his stomach turned with anxiety and disappointment.

She was with a group of yuppie/hipsters—or whatever you call people who wear fashionably expensive clothes, and look like they have money. They were yucking it up. When Sheldon arrived at their table, one of the men gave him his seat, next to Donna's.

Sallie didn't need to know anything else. He pulled out a twenty, placed it on the bar, and waved at the waitress. He ambled to the elevator, hoping he wasn't calling attention to himself, got out at the lobby and from there, climbed into a cab and returned to his empty West Village apartment where he crawled into bed wondering how it was possible that he had ever believed anything good could come from seeing Donna again. The knowledge that she was seeing Sheldon Kessler was so emotionally devastating it was hard to accept, but the facts spoke for themselves. There were coincidences in life, but he doubted the Sheldon Kessler/ Donna connection was one of them. The timing was prophetic. Clearly, someone had planned this.

17

The following morning, Sal sent his detectives to pick Ray up and have him locate his pal Matty, who, after witnessing the slice and dice incident at Kiki had mysteriously gone MIA. He figured if they got Matty to make a statement, then he could bring The Proof back in for some more Q&A.

Ted and Jackie met Ray on First Avenue, in front of the cavernous lobby of NYU Hospital and performed the perfunctory handshakes accompanied with smiles all around. It was like a family reunion.

Their first stop was a deli on Second. Ray strolled out with two liters of Coke and a Red Bull, Jackie and Teddy with coffees and a box of Krispy Kremes. After putting the goodies in the car, Ray walked back into the store for a minute before coming out again. " I got me some Advil for my pain and barbecue potato chips for my nourishment. Once the Bull and the Coke hits my system, I'll be nice and alert and the Advil, yo, that's to keep me from feeling much pain."

"You got two liters of Coke?" Jackie asked.

"Yeah, man. The first is to chase the Bull. The second is for later to keep the energy flowing."

They took the Drive South to The Brooklyn Bridge and headed through gentrified Park Slope and East along the water. All the way Ray was shouting directions. When the neighborhoods took a change for the worst, he tapped Detective Schwartz on the shoulder. "You know the Souls of Mischief "No Man's Land"? Welcome to old school Red Hook. The original land of no man."

"You from here, cowboy?" Teddy glanced at the small white dude.

"Yep. Red Hook. Me and Matty's family, we were the last of the white Mohegans."

Jackie surveyed the surroundings, "Doesn't look like too much has changed."

"Not here it hasn't, everything looks the same as it ever was."

"Yeah, man, but now you're a big time producer. You're a long ways gone."

"Not long enough. Being in this neighborhood is bringing it all back to me. And it ain't good. Back in the day, when I wasn't running for my life from the Puerto Ricans and black kids, I was running from my father, violent prick that he was."

"Oh yeah? What was he doing here?"

"Big Ray Senior, he was a part time longshoreman and full time alcoholic. Thank god for Matty. I literally couldn't have survived without him and now I'm wondering if he's survived without me."

Ray leaned forward and pointed to a dilapidated building with a bar on the ground floor. "That there's the first stop, the Emerald. That's where Matty's ma used to send us on what we called the suicide mission, bringing his six-two, three-hundred pound dad, Harry, home for dinner. What a joke!" Ray took a hit off the coke bottle. "Stop the car." He slid out and headed toward the raggedy dive. The detectives followed. Inside, the combined stench of body odor, cigarettes, and stale beer was sickening. "Hey, Lawless, that you?"

"Hey, Monty," Ray said to the sickly old man behind the bar.

"Hey kid, what's goin' on?"

"Nothin' much, Monty. Matty been in lately?" "I ain't seen Matty, but Doreen's been by." "How she doin'?"

"Same ol'. How youse been?"

Ray walked over to the old jukebox in the far corner of the narrow room "Stranger in the Night," "Hello Dolly," "Mack the Knife" and other relics of the past were on the song list. "Same old songs? Huh, Monty?"

"Same old everything, Ray."

"Let's get out of here," Ray put his hand to his forehead. "All of a sudden I'm feeling weak. He gave Monty a perfunctory "See yuh," and hustled to the street, the detectives right behind.

Standing on the on the broken sidewalk near the car, Ray pointed to an old tenement up the street.

"Doreen's Matty's mom. That's where she lives at."

The front door was open. They walked right into the bleak hallway. The dimly lit walls were decorated in eye- popping multi layers of fresh graffiti.

"She's up on the sixth floor."

Ray groaned with every step but hung tough to the end. There were four doors per landing. Ray picked the one with eight locks and started pounding on it. "Doreen? It's Ray. Open up." When there was no reply, he took off a sneaker and smacked it hard against the black painted steel. "Doreen! It's Ray. I'm lookin' for Matty."

The woman who opened the door was wrapped in a thin nylon bathrobe circa 1960; a half-smoked cigarette dangled in the Dean Martin rat-pack style from her mouth. She wasn't Marylyn or Jane Russell, but with her hair piled up old Hollywood style she could have been typecast as the cheap old broad in a late night B movie.

"Yo, Doreen, these guys here are with the police." "Oh yeah, wadda they want?"

"They're looking for Matty."

"Come in. Come in. Nobody's gonna bite ya."

A moment later they were in a linoleum floored room with ready-for-the-dumpster furniture.

Ray seemed unbearably uncomfortable as he looked around.

"Jeeze, Doreen, it's bringing back a lot of memories." "Oh yeah? Like what?"

"Like that ashtray."

"Oh that's the one I busted open Harry's jaw with." She croaked a raspy smoker's cough while a lit cigarette hung magically between her lips. "How youse doin,' Ray? Long time no see."

Ray waited. Then did the old New York thing and answered the question with a question. "How *you* doin,' Doreen?"

"Still livin' in this dump. Nobody come to rescue me yet."

"You're lookin' good, Doreen, still lookin' good." Even though they knew that etiquette required it, the detectives marveled at how sincerely the compliment was delivered. "I'm lookin' for Matty. You ain't seen him around, have ya?" "Aw, shit, Ray, and here I was thinking you was here to see *me*." She grinned and gave him a slithery slap on the arm. "What's he done now?"

"Nothin'. I'm just lookin' for him is all." Ray pulled out two twenties and laid them on the coffee table near where she was sitting.

"I ain't seen him, I told youse," she said, hissing the words as though he had insulted her.

This time when she spoke, both detectives observed a total tooth count of four. They watched as she stubbed out the butt on a beer can before dropping it into the ashtray. Then she snatched up the money and tucked it into her bra. "I always liked youse, Ray. Youse is all right."

"Tell Matty to call me," he said, as he, Jackie and Ted exited the apartment.

"Sure. I'll do that," she said. "Come again detectives." Her attempt at a seductive delivery was so old school cheesy it was almost laughable.

The cop car was right out front where it had been before they'd made the long climb to Doreen's apartment. There were fourteen steps between each landing. They'd slogged up to the fifth landing and back down in less than ten minutes. Ray took a seat and cracked the second liter of Coke.

"Where to now, Ray?" Jackie asked, turning the key in the ignition.

"Head three blocks toward the water and then one block east," Ray said. The road led them past dilapidated three- story houses and vacant lots piled with trash. Soon, they were in front of a badly-in-need-of-repair mustard-yellow two story with a white front door that had turned battered gray from the daily assault of the city's grime.

"Home sweet home, stop right here."

Before he got out of the car, Ray gave them a heads up. "The place is gonna be a pigsty. But when all systems are down, this is where Matty usually winds up. The woman who lives here is his ex-wife, Candy."

Ray got out of the car, walked to the door, and much to the amazement of both detectives, crossed himself before knocking.

"Get the fuck out of here," a female voice implored. "We don't want any."

Ray kept banging. "Candy, it's Ray." The sound of steps seemed like someone was coming to the door. "Candy, it's Ray," he said again. A skinny redhead with a rose tattoo on her neck opened the door a crack. She was blitzed.

"I'm lookin' for Matty," Ray said.

She showed no sign of recognition. "What do you want?"

"Candy, it's Ray, Matty's friend." "What do you want with Matty?"

"He's gone missin', Candy. I need to find him. Look, stay there. I'll be right back with a few beers and some butts. These guys here are cops. Okay? They're gonna watch you for a minute." Ray ran to the corner and into the deli. He returned with two six-packs of Miller and a carton of Kools and tilted the open grocery bag toward Candy so she could see that he was for real. Then she let him and the detectives in.

"Hey, Candy, what's up?" "What's up with you, Ray?"

"I ain't seen Matty around for a couple of days. You seen him?"

"Jeez, Ray, what happened to you? You're all cut up." She attempted to touch his bloody bandage.

"Yeah, Candy, I'm all cut up. Listen, have you seen Matty?"

"Are you in some kinda trouble, Ray?"

"Candy, could you *please* answer the question? These men here are police. Let's not be wasting their time, okay?"

"I don't know what ta say, Ray."

"Just answer nice and simple like. Yes if he's here, no if he isn't, and if you don't know, try saying that."

Ray got a blank stare for his effort.

"I'll try again, Candy. Please, is Matty around?"

"I ain't seen him in a while," she said. "But you can check the basement."

Ray headed directly for a door in the kitchen and threw it open. The detectives heard his hurried footsteps as he descended.

"You got any light down here, Candy?" he shouted from the bottom of the stairs.

Seconds later, the flicker of a low watt bulb shed enough light for him to see shapes on the other side of the space. As he stepped over mountains of debris the detectives followed him with their flashlights. Their lights yielded a motionless body encrusted in filth, slime, and dried up blood, spread out on a sofa. Ray put his ear to its mouth.

"Come on, Matty, wake up! It's Ray." Then he cradled his closest friend's head in his arms.

Jackie was about six feet away, standing in a foot of empty bottles and plastic bags filled with trash, his flashlight in his hand.

"He alive, Teddy?"

Ted's hand was on Matty's neck. "He's got a pulse. Better call for an ambulance, though." He moved Ray out of the way, and put his ear to his mouth. "Fuck, Jack, this kid smells like piss, shit and beer." "What kind?"

Ted fired back, "Dog, goat, domestic." "He gonna make it?" asked Ray.

"Believe me, we've seen a hell of a lot worse. Once he sobers up, he's gonna be fine."

18

Sallie leaned on the edge of his desk and faced his two detectives and a dozen street cops. He waved a handful of papers at them. "Thanks to Ted and Jackie, we got our witness. All four ex-cons are in their respective apartments. Amend that, they're in their mothers' apartments."

Sal got a big laugh.

"We had them tailed and got the reports. Seems our recidivists had themselves a night of reefer madness and extreme party play. I guess they needed it to flush out the bitter aftertaste of their first visit here. "

More laughs and a round of applause.

"Unfortunately, what they did last night to celebrate their short-lived release is going to quickly become a memory that they can savor for a long time to come during their stay in the big house." Sal glanced down at his paperwork. "You know what to do. Pick them up and get them back here. We'll be waiting for them."

When his mama shook him awake, Pea Head thought he was still dreaming. It was a bad one too. Cops were standing around his bed telling him to get dressed, before he'd even had his breakfast. "You're goin' for a little ride," they said, It was a fuckin' nightmare…except that it wasn't one. It was worse. These motherfuckin' cops were for real, big too. They even showed him their shields and shit. Okay, this was reality. He'd have to adjust. All kinds of messed- up things happened in life. Expect the un- expected, that's what he was about. Who the fuck could predict you'd be chillin' with your homies one second, firebombed the next second, put in jail, then right away get released, and then be in all the papers like you was a superstar. Oh, well. Like the rhyme goes: *Row, row, row, your boat, gently down the stream. Merrily, merrily, merrily, merrily, life is but a dream.* Why make waves?

Pea Head shuffled peacefully out of his mother's place with the officers. "See you later, Mama," he said.

Words of comfort came easily, "You be good now, son."

The cops who came for Freeze had a whole different experience. As soon as he saw them, he jetted right out of the bed, with nothing on but his clowny drawers. It was a good thing for the po-po that his mama had triple- locked the door behind them, though why you need to lock your apartment when you've got two big cops inside with you is a little incomprehensible. Maybe it was out of habit. Anyway Freeze ran half naked for the door, hoping to bust out but he couldn't figure out how to undo the locks. "Damn you, Mama," he said, turning to face the cops. He could kill somebody right now. "Get the fuck out of here, motherfuckers! I'm in the papers."

He was gonna go on about how the professor got him out and how he was innocent in the first place and then go on to the subject of police brutality—particularly against people of color—but he didn't get a chance. Rather than try to subdue him mano a mano, the motherfuckin' cowards drew their guns.

"I wouldn't do that if I were you," one of them said, waving his pistol with a finger on the trigger. "If you don't shut up and get dressed, we're gonna blow your fucking head off.' The man with the gun looked like he'd have fun doing it too. "Ever hear of resisting arrest and endangering the lives of an officer of the law?"

They looked at his mother who was averting her eyes from her son. "Sorry, ma'am," the smaller one said.

Freeze turned to his mother. "Do something, bitch," he said.

One of the cops smacked him in the head. "We're just trying to make him be respectful."

"I appreciate it, officer," she said to him. Then to her son, "You'd best be puttin' some clothes on," she said, with a calm close to beatitude. "If I was you, I'd cooperate with these gentlemen. Rantin' and ravin' like a mad cow ain't going to be doin' yoself no good."

Freeze obeyed. But he muttered a steady stream of expletives as he slow-motion-moved toward his bedroom. It was his way of fighting the power, and he was gonna fight it 'til they took all the fight from him.

While two of the cops helped him dress, he could hear mama, Clover, talking to the one by the door.

"I seen the whole thing comin'," she said. "I always knowed my son was no angel and, with the Lord's help, I come to accept it. Not an easy thing to do. At first, his misbehavin' done drive me to the drink. I never left this place 'cept to walk to the liquor store. My cousin, Yvonne, she hate what she was seein'. That sweet, sweet woman gettin' sick over somethin she can't control,' she say. Yvonne and my other cousin, her sister Dee, do one a those interventions on me."

"Keep quiet, old woman," Freeze glowered, while pulling on his sneakers. "No one's listenin'."

Clover ignored him. "One day they come over with a pastor and he and all a them lay hands on me, tell me how much they love me and how I need a change. Every day after that, Yvonne, she take me to those AA meetin's, and Sundays, she take me to her church where that pastor praised the Lord for bringin' sister Clover to their house of worship. That was four years ago, gentlemen, and I'm still good."

Science met the officers with a smile and held out his wrists. "You here to cuff me?" he said. "So be it." The reading of the rights, the cuffs on the wrist, the walk to the car, the gentle way one of the city's finest protected his head from bumping against the roof of the car, all went so well like that, to an observer, it seemed almost choreographed.

Scholar heard a commotion outside and pulled the lace curtain back from the window to see what it was about. "What the hell!" he said half asleep, half stoned from the night before. He made a beeline for his bedroom window at the back of the apartment. There was no way he was about to make it easy for the cops. He had his reputation to consider. There was not a molecule of submissiveness in his entire physiology. As he unlocked the latch and tugged the window open, he suddenly paused with one leg hanging over the edge of the sill. What was he thinking? He couldn't go anywhere. He was nine stories up. If he jumped, there'd be pieces of him all over the playground.

The officers wasted no time in kicking open his flimsy-ass Section 8 bedroom door. The first man in said, "Make my day, asshole. Go ahead and jump," as he waved his gun at him.

The officer directly behind him put salt in the wound. "No sweat off our balls, Scholar. Ready for blastoff when you are."

Scholar was fuming, yo. Wasn't it highly unprofessional for them to encourage a suicide? As unprofessional as those cops who had firebombed him and then started shooting. The NYPD was out of control. He needed to assert himself. "Fuck you, stupid motherfuckers."

"Did you hear that Raul? Look who he's calling stupid?" The first officer was laughing. "He's standing near a window, threatening to jump, and we're stupid." He directed his next sentence at Scholar like Scholar was his bitch. "Okay, Tinkerbell, get dressed and let's get out of here. Your pals are waiting for us down at the station."

Tinkerbell? He could take going back to jail, but no one had the right to call him a faggot. That was too much for Scholar, and he full on went at the man.

The cop called Raul decked him with his stick and, while he was on the floor, clamped the cuffs on him. Scholar bitched and cussed, but the officers weren't impressed. They dressed him in some mismatched clothes to humiliate him and put his ass in the car without even giving him the courtesy of protecting his head from knocking hard into the roof. "Bitches!" he yelled just in case anyone who mattered was listening. He wanted it to be known he ain't go down without a fight.

Slumped in the backseat of the squad car, Scholar peered out the window and thought about the ordeal to come. Unfortunately, he couldn't shut out the voice of his chauffeur in blue, on his mike with the volume of the outside speaker turned up blasting. "Woof, woof, woof," he howled. It was pumped up so loud, it made Scholar wince. Then the officer turned around, winked at his prisoner and said off mic, "Who's the bitch now, Tinkerbell?"

MARC BLATTE

19

Now that the homies were back in the station, Sallie felt giddy at the prospect of finally getting to the bottom of what had happened at the Kiki. He decided he'd start with the hardest nut to crack. "Welcome back, Freeze. It's good to see you again. Kind of like homecoming week in high school, which I guess you wouldn't know about since you never went. Can I get you something?"

"Look, man. This shit is gettin' old. What for you got me here this time?"

"I got a witness that says you were the man who used a box cutter and put a young gentleman in the hospital."

"That's bullshit."

"You're saying the witness is making this up?"

"No. I ain't sayin' that, but I am sayin' he seriously mistaken."

"Were you at the Kiki last Saturday night?"

"Where?"

"You know, Freeze, you're right. This *is* getting old." Sallie turned to the attending officer. "Carl, would you kindly escort him back to his new home and send in Scholar." While he waited for the transition to take place, Sallie thumbed through the papers on the desk.

Scholar pimp-rolled into the room and slid onto the chair opposite him while Sallie followed him through narrowed eyes. "How you doing?"

"Man, you like a dog with a bone," Scholar said. "You tenacious, like you onto somethin' and you ain't lettin' go."

"You look a little stressed, Scholar. I'm surprised."

Scholar'd watched enough Charlie Rose to know to say, "It's a pleasure to be back." But it was facetious.

"This must all seem like *déjà vu* for you, but hang in there with me." Sallie took a sip of coffee. "Know why you're here?"

"No, Sir. I haven't the foggiest." Again facetious.

"I hear you've been hanging out in rather exclusive company." Seeing that Scholar appeared to be confused, Sallie waited. He waited until Scholar shifted on his chair and defensively crossed his arms. "You want some Fiji water or something? I hear that's what they're drinking in the Hamptons these days."

"Who said anything about the Hamptons. I ain't know nothing 'bout no Hamptons." This was said with a little less attitude—more like the old Scholar that Sallie knew and loved.

"That's not what I hear."

"Well, you're misinformed."

"Misinformed, huh? You know, when you first came in this morning you seemed a little angry. Did something happen to upset you?"

"Whatever, man."

"You sure you won't have some Perrier or some *foie gras*? I hear there's a small bistro over on Third and Nineteenth that makes their own. Might even come from Long Island geese."

"Since you aksed, I'll have a coffee and Danish"

"Okay. Sounds good." Sallie put in his request.

He waited some more, studying Scholar like he would an abstract expressionist painting. He needed to understand the motivations that went into the creation of the object by examining the object itself. "Ya know, Scholar, I saw someone's picture in the paper. I think you might know him."

"That was me, yo. I was in the paper."

"That was you? You *were* with Professor Parks? Wow. I guess that makes you a celebrity." Sallie tapped his pencil on the tabletop several times and saw Scholar's eyes follow the movement. "You know Kal Kessler?"

"Who? Don't know who you mean, man."

"Hmm. Last time we met, you were more forthcoming. I remember you telling me that you had been at the Kiki with your posse. I don't know. Today I'm seeing all sorts of red flags waving at me from your side of the table." Sal took another sip of coffee. Then waited. When Scholar didn't respond, Sallie said, "You know who I mean. Kal. The managing agent of the housing projects where you live."

"Man, I don't know what you talkin' 'bout."

Sallie rubbed his forehead. "Look, Scholar, once again, you're hurting my feelings by playing me for an idiot. Remember when we discussed the meaning of rhetorical questions? I am asking you rhetorical questions. I already know the answers. You know Kal Kessler. You give him drugs, which he takes with great pleasure and frequency. You and him party with your crack-whores in the Hamptons." Sallie rubbed his nose and leaned back in his chair. "You think when a guy who looks like you goes to Citarella or the Jewelry Exchange or Gucci people don't notice? Everybody and his brother notice you. You're like a circus freak out there. You might as well put one of the stupid signs on your back that says, drugs for sale, dealer, thief, burglar here."

Scholar put a leg on his knee and clasped it with both hands. It was shaking like a leaf in a hurricane. "Okay. What you want?" he said.

"I want to know who cut Ray." From the look on Scholar's face, Sallie knew the young degenerate had caught a glimpse of the future and could see the large ever-giving titty of sustenance moving further and further into the distance. Soon it would be out of reach.

Sallie applied his Liquid Wrench, the absence of sound, knowing that by remaining silent the truth that was stuck somewhere between Scholar's scheming brain and active mouth would come loose and spill out. Then sure enough....

"Man, it happen so fast, I can't recollect." Scholar had both feet on the floor now and was shaking his head.

"What happened so fast, Scholar?"

"Man, why you playin' me like this? This is rhetorical bullshit. You the man wit the answers. What's in it for me anyways?"

"I'll talk to the DA and maybe he'll let you slide."

"I don't want no maybes. I want it in writin', yo."

"Okay. I'll get it for you, in exchange for testimony. Now, what happened at the Kiki between you and Ray that night?"

"That punk come over to us. Start tellin' us we was unprofessional. Ain't got no skills. Gettin' up in our face."

"Back up a minute. How did you know Ray?"

"We met at his reckit label."

"What label is that?"

"Elektrik Records."

"What happened there?"

"Yo, man, you really give a fuck what happen there?"

"I sure do." Sallie drank the rest of his cold coffee and tossed the cup into the wastebasket.

Scholar folded his hands on the table and stared at them while talking. "We up there chillin' wit Sunn Volt, the owner of Elektrik. We play him our joint. He love it, man. Talkin' 'bout how he was gonna sign us up. Then this punk ass producer come over and Sunn play him only a minute of our joint before he say, 'Sunn, I ain't feelin' this.' All disrespectful. Know what I'm sayin'?"

Sallie nodded. "Then what happened?"

"We leave, but first Sunn give us an invite to his party."

"Then you saw this guy Ray there."

"Correct. We see Ray."

"Right."

"Well...Ray, he come over to us like he the man. He say, 'What you doin' here?' Pea Head say, 'Sunn put us on the guest list.' Then he smile and shake his head like Sunn had made some kind a mistake. So I say, 'Hey, man, why you do us like that yesterday up at Elektrik?' Ray say, 'Look, man. You wants to be playas, but you ain't got skills. Your shit was pathetic. If Biz wasn't your cuz, you wouldn't a gotten past the front door.' Science was 'bout to deck the motherfucker, but I held him back. I despise violence, yo."

Sallie nodded and chewed on the inside of his cheek.

"Then Ray say, 'Come on, bitch,' all up in Science's face. Meanwhile, this other white motherfucker, all tatted up, lookin' like a Hell's Angel say, 'You all can kiss my cracker ass.' Next thing I know, Science, he on the floor all doubled over, while this biker boy is stompin' on him. I try to intercede, but to no avail, yo. The Angel dude must a been on crystal meth or some shit. You know how they do. Then he pulls a knife and one thing leads to another and Freeze is defending himself with a cheesy little box cutter, but Sunn's boy Ray gets in the middle of it."

Sallie locked hands behind his head and widened his eyes. "Wow. You're lucky to be alive, Scholar."

"Word. Thank God." Scholar lifted his right hand in praise.

"You think this Hell's Angel would have killed you?" Sallie spoke in a grave tone, as if everything Scholar had described actually happened.

"Mos' def," Scholar said. "No doubt 'bout it. Me or Science, Freeze... any one of us. The man was dusted or somethin', yo. That shit can fuck a man up."

"If I showed you a picture, you think you could identify him?"

"Worth a try. I'm cooperatin' as best I can." Scholar 's tone was a good imitation of sincerity.

Sallie opened a folder. "So, you're willing to testify that it was Freeze who sliced and diced Ray."

"Yes, sir. But it was a accident."

"Scholar, let's keep this simple," Sallie said, exasperated by the game. "Forget the accident bullshit. I know there were no Hell's Angels at the Kiki. The white boy with Ray was a skinny little twerp. He told us the whole story. We got witnesses who saw it go down and they said the same thing he did. You guys beat the shit out of Ray, and one of you sliced him. You know it. I know it. Case closed."

Scholar's eyes darted around the room and then focused on the ceiling. He scratched his chin and then rubbed his face. "I tried to stop him, yo. But a man can only do what he can do. Right, detective?"

"If you say so, Scholar. You can go now." Sallie turned to the officer in attendance. "Bring Freeze back in here."

Several minutes later, Freeze slid onto the still warm chair, carrying a carton of milk. Sallie took a good look at him. Scary, his piercing eyes, tall lanky body, and predator posture all telegraphed, "Don't mess with me." He placed the milk carton on the table.

Sallie sat on the other side of the table facing him. "Here we are again," he said. "Another get-together due to a silly misunderstanding. Can I get you something? I know how hungry a young man can get waiting around."

"You got a sandwich or something like dat?"

"I can get you one, Freeze. What kind would you like?"

"How 'bout a bacon and egg on toast?"

"Sure. How you like the eggs?"

"Scrambled."

Sal nodded to the attendant.

"Last time you were here, we talked a little about the Kiki Club. This time, we have witnesses who have given statements as to what happened that night."

Freeze pushed at the cuticle on his thumbnail. "Yeah? Well, folks talk."

"True, but we deal in facts here. Given the fact that we found the weapon on you in the parking lot and the weapon had blood from the victim, what people are saying can be pretty damaging."

"Look, man. Dat ain't my cutter, and I ain't done no one wit it."

"Your fingerprints were all over it."

"Professor Parks 'n me been down dis road. You can't use dat as evidence."

"Scholar just told me you cut the kid."

Freeze looked like he'd been zapped by a stun gun. "Scholar don't know shit!"

Sallie dug in and got right up in Freeze's face. "What Scholar doesn't know doesn't mean shit to me. I only know he's willing to *say* he knows in a court of law. And believe me, I know other people who will testify to the same thing."

"You talkin' 'bout Pea Head and Science?"

"Could be." Sallie decided he wouldn't mention Matty.

"Those punk ass motherfuckers."

"Think about what I'm telling you, Freeze."

Freeze sat on the edge of his chair and stared confidently into Sallie's eyes. "Listen up, yo. How 'bout this? I got some shit to tell you gonna change everything. But I ain't sayin' nothing 'less I know I can walk."

"That's a promise I can't make. You nearly killed a man while you were on parole. That's big."

"Well, this is bigger. Come on man, give me somethin'." "Let's hear what you've got. If it's good, I'll try to work something out."

Freeze had his poker face on. Sallie scanned it for a sign of what might come, but it told him nothing. "That big white dude that got killed at Kiki? That was Scholar did him."

"Why would Scholar do that?"

"Don't know."

"Did he know him?"

"Man, I don't know. All I knows is we was parked up the block. Scholar gets outta the car, says he got some business to attend to. I see him leave, den I get out to see what he up to. He wastes dat big dude, try to kill the other one look just like him, but dat one run away."

"Which way did he run?"

"Over toward Fifth."

"Did Scholar follow him?"

"Hell no. Scholar, he just come back."

"Then what happened?"

"He gets in the car like nuttin' happen."

"Did you see a gun?"

"You mean when he gets back in da car?"

"Yeah?"

"No, but I might have."

"Let's stick with what you saw. What happened after that?"

"We just drive on back to Far Rock like nuttin' happened."

"Nobody said anything about the shots? The guys must have heard something."

"The radio was blastin', yo. Ain't nobody hear nothin'."

Sallie visualized the sequence of events as Freeze had explained them. The pieces fit. "What time was it?" he asked.

"Four-thirty, somethin' like dat."

Sallie stuck out his bottom lip and narrowed his eyes. "Anybody else see it happen?"

"I ain't see nobody."

"What about Pea Head and Science?"

"No, man. Dey was chillin' in the car with the music on, like I said."

"You know anyone named Kal?"

"Who he?"

"If you don't know him, it doesn't matter."

"He a white boy?"

"Yeah."

"I know Scholar been hangin' wit some white boy."

"What's he look like?" Sallie sat forward on the edge of his chair and fiddled with his pencil. "Money."

Back at his desk, Sallie had a sit-down with Ted and Jackie. "I'm going in there again with Scholar for round two in a minute, but something's still not clear. If Scholar shot Pashko, why? And who ran down Vooko, and why'd they do that? And we still don't know who shot Donny."

Jackie pulled on his right earlobe while focusing on the pink-flowered box of Kleenex on Sallie's desk. "Freeze says Scholar shot Pashko, but he also says Scholar didn't know him. Suppose that's true. Why would Scholar shoot him, if he doesn't even know the guy?"

"Shekels," Ted said.

Jackie gave him a sideways glance. "And if Scholar shot Donny, too. Why?"

"Same thing. He needed money, Jack."

Sallie shook his head. "Money for what? I find it hard to believe that Scholar would target a big-time attorney for cash...and how could he get it from him, if the guy's dead? Scholar fucks up and kills Pashko, when

Vooko is the intended target. That I can buy, but why is Vooko the target? If it's true that Scholar and Kal have been hanging out together at the Hamptons, it's possible their connection involves more than drugs. I'm thinking maybe Kal wanted to get back at Vooko for the public humiliation at the club the previous week. People have been killed for a lot less, I guess. But Kal would have no reason for having Donny whacked. He was a personal friend and his family's attorney."

"Jealousy," Jackie said. "You saw the picture in the paper—Sheldon and Donny in the foreground having a ball and Kal slinking around in back."

The detectives sat in silence. Finally, Ted said, "I'm not saying that's not possible, Jackie, But check this out. Donny's Audi is found in the lot, twenty feet away from where Pashko is shot. We call him. His alibi is that he was with Leah Kessler all evening. Kal's alibi is that he was with the two of them. Of course Kal is probably full of shit. So let's say, wherever he was is still an unknown."

"I like that, muscle man," Sallie said. " now you're talking sense."

20

In the article about the attorney Donovan, there was a lot of information to do with the Kesslers that Vooko found illuminating. Things like how much Sheldon's real estate empire was worth. It reported that, in addition to his apartment in the Dakota—the famous building that was home to John Lennon—the family had an estate in East Hampton, a ski house in Beaver Creek, a house in Palm Beach, and one on some island called St. Bart's. Vooko found it hard to get his head around this kind of wealth. Where he was from, no one had more than one house and it was usually packed to overflowing with extended family members who had lost theirs.

He had read about East Hampton in glossy magazines like *Source* and *Vibe*, but he'd never had any interest in actually going there before. Now, he was curious. The impression he got was that the folks out there had it going on for real, unlike say the Jersey Shore, where the vibe was definitely low rent…a cheap imitation. With all the shit that was exploding in his head, he could use some downtime. He'd never been to East Hampton. Why not check it out?

Vooko hit Pelham Parkway around noon. Traffic was way light. By 1:30, he was off the LIE and on a two-lane heading east. The land was soccer-field flat and there were actually a few farms! He hadn't seen a farm in years. Not since he'd left his village. He scanned the fields for signs of domesticated animals, like pigs and chickens and maybe a cow, but didn't see any. Farms without animals; what did the farmers eat? America was indeed a land of mystery.

He was on Route 27 heading east just past a place called Once Upon A Bagel, whatever the fuck that was supposed to mean, in a town called

Wainscott. Vooko pulled off the road into a small shopping mall to check his location. The map made it look like East Hampton was less than ten miles away.

Back on track and cruising nicely to a love jam by that child snatcher R. Kelly, he scanned the horizon. What was with the super-sized cribs on the dirt fields? Farmhouses? Damn. He had heard farming was big business with government subsidies and all. Strange. And why, he wondered, would anyone want to build a big house on the edge of a dirt field? It would always be dusty. And what about the noise? Tractors working just outside the house would be loud and annoying...and the smell! Fertilizer was cow shit. Now that was something he knew about, and no way was he gonna have it fumigating his crib. He had heard the expression "the rich are not like you and me," but the Hamptons...damn! Must be an example of just how different they were. And anyway, where were the cows?

Route 27 took him to a sign that said Village of East Hampton, and underneath, *founded in 1648*. His Gucci knockoff told him that he was only slightly over two hours from the Boogie Down. The magnificent old trees, with their newly sprouted soft green leaves, lining both sides of the roadside were awesome. So were the graceful swans gliding in the pond he was passing. The old churches, the cemetery, and the stone buildings he saw were older than anything he'd seen yet in this new-fangled country of his. The whole thing looked authentic, solid, like you could make a real life for yourself here. When he came to the pretty white library with the American flag in front of it he actually got a lump in his throat. Goosebumps. yo. He was feeling all mushy like when Ray Charles sang that song "Oh beautiful for spacious skies" on the Superbowl or some shit. He was believing in freedom and tolerance and other high-minded things that he'd heard this country was all about. Word, he had been living in the US of A for fourteen years and finally he had discovered America!

Coming into what looked like the main part of town, he saw several pedestrians move slowly across the street. In the city they would be dead meat, but here traffic stopped and nobody honked their car horns at them...unbelievable. These American people were polite, considerate, it wasn't all about themselves. Different.

At the first light, he hung a left and found a long street with one small retail shop lined up after the other. He eyed a sign saying COFFEE and an open parking spot right in front of it. He pulled in and turned off the car engine. Man, he had to check this town out! Why the fuck not? The sun was shining, he could smell a slightly salty aroma in the air, and everything in the town was like a post card, picture perfect, yo.

In the café, near his parking space, Vooko ordered his usual double latte with soy milk. The Mexican girl behind the counter served him efficiently and with a friendly smile. The coffee was just like he liked it. No doubt about it, the taste and texture of the latte equaled that of any at Starbucks. He took his drink and strolled around town. Many of the cars parked at the curbs or driving past him were foreign— Range Rovers, BMWs, Volvos and Mercedes seemed to predominate. For the most part, they looked brand new. The clothes displayed in the store windows were not exactly his style, but he recognized the designer names on the labels... Ralph Lauren, Coach, Armani, Kate Spade, Gucci, and Kenneth Cole.

Thinking this town might be a good place for him to eventually settle, he stopped to peer into the window of one of the many real estate agents. The least expensive houses pictured were over eight hundred thousand dollars, and they resembled the unsubstantial development homes he'd seen from the Jersey Turnpike. Houses in the million dollar range were more suitable. The ones that had his name on them, though, were over seven mill.

The one that really caught his eye didn't even have a price on it. *Why bother putting it in the window yo, if they ain't even gonna tell me how much it is?* He didn't get it, and not getting it made him feel a little unnerved. So Vooko returned to his car to get his bearings, chill a bit, and study the printout of the directions he had downloaded from the cybercafé near his apartment.

Soon, he was zipping by a golf course and some of the biggest houses he had ever seen. This place was the deal! No doubt about it. When he became a mega-millionaire, he was gonna be right here, in his twenty-eight bedroom, subtly pimped-out crib. Word up, yo! He'd even play golf and invite his rich neighbors over for cocktails or whatever they did when the weather was good and they wanted to get a buzz on. And he would be more flexible about the threads he styled in. If the locals wore Ralph Lauren preppy shit, so would he. Pink shirts with little alligators, green pants, and even those whack lids. He was down. Fuck it, he'd go all the way, bro, and get himself those stupid-ass shoes called docksiders, and start parting his thick black hair on the side and over, nice and white-bread like they did out here. It would probably make him look like he fit in better than with his current, swept back Scarface style. After all, wasn't he a when-in-Rome type guy?

He had no problem finding the Kessler mansion. How could he miss it? The oval sign jutting from the white post announced this was GOLDEN POND FARM and below, in much smaller print, THE KESSLERS.

Vooko didn't stop or turn into the driveway, though. Now, if he were cruisin' in a Benz S class, that would have been a whole other story. He would have pulled that bad boy right up to the motherfuckin' house and represented. But he wasn't, so he kept driving up the road another quarter of a mile to a more secluded wooded area and pulled over into a little gravel parking lot of some kind of wildlife preserve.

Golden Pond Farm was set back a good ways from the road. Most of the land was emerald green grass broken up by an occasional mighty oak tree lookin' old as the planet. The sprawling home was red brick. It looked very Masterpiece Theater, English country style, maximum chill.

Since he was wearing his tracksuit and sneakers, and had seen several joggers on the road, he set off up the driveway toward the house in a casual trot. When he got close to the front door he made a little show of stretching, like he was just another trustafarian doin' his exercise thing on this perfect spring day.

He took a walk around the property and he felt every inch of it. The tennis courts had his name all over them. The pool too, and it wasn't no ordinary pool neither. It blended in to the natural setting like it was belonged. Check it: with ridiculous big boulders and a Tarzan movie waterfall, it could have been a Hollywood set. Oh, did he wish he had his camera and that Pashko were still alive! He would feel it just like Vooko did. This was fucked up yo, one of those Kodak moments, but no one he loved to share it with.

"May I help you, young man?"

A scrawny wino-looking old white guy with a rake in his hand was talking to him. Vooko could smell liquor on his breath all the way from where he was standing.

"Yes sir, I'm a friend of Kal's. He told me to stop by when I was in the Hamptons." He made his voice sound like one of those fake ass intellectual people he and Pashko used to love to make fun of on CSPAN.

"He's not home right now."

"That's too bad." Looking behind the man past the gurgling pool water he saw a humongous garage.

"Can I help you with something."

Vooko pointed to it. "Kal had a car he was looking to sell. Do you mind if I take a look?" He counted seven separate car ports.

"I don't have the keys." The man gave him a dumb stare.

Lazy, lying ass motherfucker, Vooko thought, which he locked down tight so as not to let it reach his lips. Instead he said in his best use-a-multi-syllable-word-when a-simple- one-will-do-fine, CSPAN style, "I appreciate your help. Thank you."

"Okey doke." The old Yankee said. "Have a good one."

"Have one, yourself." He had just reminded himself of Steve Martin or Chevy Chase, two of the most pissed off, Republican-looking, white guys ever. Among other things he had learned from watching their ridiculous funny movies is that in speaking American English there are a multitude of ways of saying fuck you without saying it. Like maybe saying okey doke in a real sincere type way.

Vooko ran up the loose gravel driveway and back on the public road toward his car. A couple was jogging in the opposite direction. The man was rail thin, maybe sixty, maybe nine hundred, Vooko couldn't tell, but he had a sense that in his ratty-ass, faded sweats with Princeton written in super-large print, the man was representing. Vooko had seen Princeton brand clothes once or twice at the Kiki, the folks wearing them had a look of belonging about them, like they owned the world and everybody else was renting space. Personally he identified himself with the Nike brand.

The woman running behind had a tight face and straight blond hair pulled back with a black headband. Vooko dug her big pearl earrings and especially got off on the way she went ugh, ugh, ugh every time she took a step, in that triple X-rated, for adults only, movie way, like she was getting low and dirty and shit. Very sexy.

He slowed down to a leisurely walk when he hit the parking lot, then went into the reserve and headed in the same direction he had just come from. The path he was on led him to within visual range of the back of the garage. He was here to check the place out and no lazy ass, wino gardener was gonna keep him from it. In the distance, he could see a mini version of the big house. Maybe a guesthouse, he thought, nice, but reconsidered when he saw a white fence with two horses roaming inside. Yeah, it was a barn. Word! This joint was next level! Incomprehensible.

Protected by a stone wall that went from a wooded area to the back driveway, he was able to move unseen to the monster-size garage. The building's sparkly clean windows allowed him to take a peek at what sort of bad-ass machines big money bought. Damn! He saw an old Bentley. Classic. He had no idea of the year. The hood ornament would look hot dangling from a silver chain, yo, but that was for another day when he was rolling in the do re mi and could pop for it no problem. As if the Bentley weren't enough for the Kesslers, he counted two BMW roadsters, a Mercedes sedan and a black Lincoln Navigator.

As he stared at the Navigator, he was hit with a flashback. A car exactly like it had almost killed him about ten days ago. What was up with that? Could this car be the same one that had sent him to the hospital? He shaded his eyes from the sun's glare and focused on the front end, but it was impossible to see anything. His heart was racing. Somehow, he had to get a closer look.

He took a stone from the wall then tapped as quietly as he could against one of the glass panes. After only two little hits, he had a gap barely large enough for a couple of his long fingers to get to the lock. Lightning-fast, he unlatched it, pushed up the window, and climbed through.

Dropping onto the floor of the garage, he paused to listen for any sound indicating a guard was on to him. He heard nothing but birds and, far in the distance, the barking of a dog. He crept over to the Navigator.

"I thought I told you to stay out of here."

It was wino the gardener. Seein' that lyin' motherfucker made him mad crazy.

"You lyin' bitch. You said you didn't have a key." Vooko walked right toward the man as if he were going to kill him.

"I did?" The man was terrified.

"Don't act all innocent with me." Vooko lifted him up by the front of the man's shabby coat. "Here I am, a friend of Kal's, and you wouldn't even budge your drunken self to let me in to see the car that he sent me here to see. You're done. I'm telling Kal to fire your ass."

"I'm sorry, sir."

Vooko looked into the man's eyes with pure loathing. He rested them there until wino started to squirm. Vooko let go. The man fell like a sack, which was when Vooko kicked the ground and raised a little dust up in the wino man's large red nose, sending him into a coughing fit.

"Keep your ass right there. I've got to take a look at something." He walked over to the big SUV.

The passenger side and the backseat were in perfect condition. The grill in the front had no dents or scratches. But the driver's side...now that was a whole other story. The mirror was cracked and the front fender was all dented up.

Vooko froze in place, inspecting the damage again, just with his eyes, taking care not to touch any part of the vehicle. He didn't want his fingerprints on it. That was for amateurs. Eyes closed, he recreated a mental picture of the moment just before he had felt the impact that had sent him flying in the air. In his mind, he conjured up the Navigator speeding toward him, and was transported back to that instant from that night when he had peered into the windshield, wondering, for one small fraction of a second, who was trying to run him down. Now, he saw him again. He had a clear picture in his mind. It was that twitchy dude with the fine ass sister. That bitch...*Kal Kessler!*

Now that Vooko knew for sure who had tried to do him in, that little prick could kiss his twitchy little rich boy ass good-bye, for fuckin' ever.

"All right. I'm gonna let it slide", he said as he walked past the man who hadn't moved from the place he'd been told to remain in. "Yo, but don't you say a thing, or I'll be back for your sorry ass. I don't think you want that."

"No, sir."

"Alright then, have a nice day." At that moment, Vooko was. Why not spread the love?

MARC BLATTE

21

Sallie shut the door of the Buddha's office. "Captain, the shit's about to hit the fan."

"I hope it's their shit and not ours, Sallie. What have you got for me?"

"Neil just called. The Lincoln that hit Vooko was found on the Kessler Estate yesterday."

The Buddha snapped a pencil in half and threw the pieces across the room. They landed smoothly into the open wastepaper basket. "Have you contacted the East Hampton police?"

"Absolutely not. That's why I'm here talking to you."

"Okay. Bear with me while I repeat what I think has happened, in a non-sequential way." The captain was writing something in his pad. "For the time being, Sunn Volt is a happy camper, because we've got the perps that cut up his producer, Ray Lawless. Right?"

"Right."

"They're not going anywhere now. We don't have police brutality, Molotov cocktail, shoot-first-ask-question-later stories about to come out in the paper?" The Buddha threw Sal a searing look. "The professor is history."

"From what I hear, he's under control. Sunn's taken care of that."

"Good. A well-fed man is a quiet man." The captain paused while he rubbed his dome. "So the real issue is... who killed Pashko?"

"Well, that is an issue, sir." "We got Scholar on that one?"

"Yes, sir, sort of, unless Freeze is lying, and Kessler did it." "What did the kid from Pelham Parkway say?"

"He didn't say. But he's the one that told Neil about the Navigator."

"The Navigator that clipped him?" "Correct."

"How did he find out about that?" "We don't know."

"You better be able to fill in the blanks, Sallie. I feel like my ass is halfway out the window and downtown's waiting to watch it take a fast fall to the ground. Did anyone see the Navigator hit him?"

"Yes, sir. We have a witness. He didn't see who was driving, but he saw the car." Sallie tried to sound convincing, but he knew he hadn't pulled it off.

"Don't tell me." Buddha shook his head and then buried his face in his hands. "The witness is a lawyer."

"He's a little more trustworthy than that."

"Okay, Sallie, he's an ex-con."

"Why do you say that?"

The captain laughed and fell back in his chair. "I thought it was a joke, but by the look on your face, I guess it's not."

"Correct, sir. He's a car thief on parole."

"We're gonna take on the Kesslers with *that?* Are you out of your mind, Sallie? If Sheldon Kessler finds out about this, he won't let us get within a mile of his kid."

"I was thinking that maybe if we had the car that whacked the bouncer in our possession, we could run with it."

"I don't know, Sallie. We got an elephant in Kessler. So far, it sounds like a pea- shooter is all we have to take him down with. You ever try to bring an elephant down that way?"

"I agree, sir. It seems a little early in the game."

"The kid's using. Right, Sallie? And we've got his dealer locked up. Have your guys tail him. See what happens. He needs drugs, which means he's bound to score. When we catch him at it, we'll take him down."

Jackie shivered and jammed his hands into his leather jacket pockets. "This is the creepiest place in all of New York. Man, look at all these ramshackle bungalows, and those crackheads all over. Looks third world."

Teddy pulled their unmarked car into the only remaining space on the block.

"Teddy man, we're way too far away. I'm gonna get out and see what's up with our boy."

"What do you want me to do?"

"Sit tight, and try not to look white." Jackie hit his partner in the arm.

"How close are you gonna get?"

"As close as I can." Jackie opened the door. "Okay, big man. Watch my back."

Jackie did a casual stroll up the block and sat himself down across the narrow street. The man was so nonchalant, anyone watching would have thought the young detective was an old time resident. He sat down two doors from the action. Close enough to hear what was happening to the poor rich kid.

"Yo, white boy, what you want around here?" Kessler was on the porch of the house. One of a group of the neighborhood kids hanging out was raggin' on him. Like everywhere else in this segregated part of the city, some bigmouth always had something to say.

"Yo, you must be lost or crazy."

In about three seconds a muscle boy with a Yankee hat came out of nowhere and bitch-slapped the inhospitable resident upside the head.

"Are you disrespecting, punk?"

"No, man, no disrespect," the skinny, pimply kid responded.

Jackie watched as Yankee-hat stared down pimples, and BOOM! sucker-punched a big kid standing right next to him. The big one fell to the ground gagging, the wind knocked out of him.

"Why you do him like that, yo?" Pimples said. "He ain't done nothin' to you."

"Yo, man," he said. "You fuck wit my bidness," his eyes were on Kal, "You be fuckin' with me."

"He ain't done nuttin.'"

"Well, next time y'all don't do nuttin' like you did nuttin' this time, I'm gonna take your pimply lil' ass out. I ain't playin,' y'all." Then he looked around at the other kids, who in a sign of absolute submission, had their eyes fixed on the pavement. "That goes for all o' y'all. Hear?"

Dead silence. The only thing Jackie heard after that was the crashing waves on the beach less than two hundred yards to the south.

"Punk-ass," Kal's defender then took a ten-dollar bill and threw it down on the ground in the middle of the group. "Aiight now," he said, as if nothing had happened. "Go get some pizza or something. All y'all just get the fuck out of here."

Jackie headed around the back and hid in a bush behind the bungalow. Through a crack below the window frame he could see Kal walk over to a trashy-looking, tall skinny dude. The man handed Kal a baggie with white stuff in it.

"That all you got?" Kal asked.

"It's all I got. Gimme eight."

Kal reached into his back pocket and started counting hundreds. His hands were shaking so badly, it took him three tries to count to the magic number they'd agreed on. The man grabbed the money from him and counted it himself.

"You're short a hundred," the dealer said.

Jackie watched as Kal gave him another hundred.

"Thanks," Kal told the dealer as he pocketed the drugs. "I appreciate it."

Jackie heard the man laugh. "No problem." Then he addressed someone that he couldn't see. "Harold, see that this man has no problems getting to his ride."

From a hundred yards away, Ted saw Kal walk out the door. Once on the sidewalk, Kal rushed to his Aston, got in, locked up, and looked around. Then, he moved the car down the street closer to the boardwalk, away from the bungalows.

Jackie came back just in time to see Kal take a hit off the twizzle stick inside the car. "Jesus, Ted. Look at that kid. I actually feel sorry for him."

"Save it for me, Jackie. You see me driving a car like that?"

They watched as Kal turned the engine on. Ted and Jackie could hear the Beasties blasting from the car stereo as the Aston turned around then shot past them.

Ted and Jackie put the red lights on and followed with sirens blaring.

"I don't think he's stopping, Ted."

Kal was way ahead of them, speeding in and out of traffic under the nearby elevated train tracks.

"This guy's seen too many friggin' action movies. Shit, Ted, we're gonna lose him!"

"I'm going as fast as I can. What the fuck is that?"

Teddy could barely make it out, but in the distance it looked like a maroon Toyota was in front of Kal's speeding Aston. When the Aston went left, the little car ahead cut left. When it suddenly changed direction, the car kept it in check. The Japanese machine would not let Kal get past it. "What the fuck does the Toyota think he's doing."

"I don't know, Ted, but it's all good to me."

The Toyota had slowed Kal down enough to allow Ted and Jackie to get inches from the Aston's bumper. Jackie picked up the mike and put the speaker volume all the way up. "This is the NYPD. Stop the car. I repeat, stop the car."

They saw his brake lights flash momentarily but then he must have had a change of heart because he rammed his Aston into the little car ahead. The Toyota hung tough and hit the brakes. The Aston had nowhere to go and came to a halt. The front door opened, Kal jumped out waving a gun and heading toward the direction of the ocean five blocks away.

Ted and Jack followed in their car. Kal was fast, and the fact that he had a gun in his hand and drugs tweaking his brain made them keep their distance. From two blocks away, they saw Kal run behind a brick wall. They got out of the car and followed until shots were fired. Then they dove for cover behind a crumpled dumpster.

"You believe this guy, Teddy? The little fuck is actually shooting at us."

Teddy was laughing like crazy.

Jackie didn't get it. "We're getting shot at and you're laughing. What the fuck is wrong with you?"

"You call that getting shot at, Jackie? He isn't even close." Teddy tried to catch his breath. "I'm sorry, Jack, no, I can't believe this kid."

Jackie looked down at his weapon. "This is whack. What do you want to do?"

"Let's wait a minute and see what happens."

A very long minute passed then a very high, nervous voice was heard from behind the wall. "Okay, okay. Okay, okay."

"Must be Kal," Ted whispered.

Jackie took stock of where they were. "Must be, Teddy. Dog shit and garbage don't talk like that."

"Drop the gun, Kal. Come out where we can see you."

The little boy was a sorry sight, all disheveled and dirty. "Okay, okay. Okay, okay."

His hands were in the air. Ted and Jackie were moving slowly toward him. But, as soon as they got about fifty feet away, he bolted.

The advantage was Kal's, for about twenty yards. Then he started to hyperventilate. He stopped and turned his head and projectile vomited toward the detectives who were just a few feet away.

"Kal, you're one sick motherfucker," Jackie said from a safe distance, then offered instructions. "Until you're finished puking, turn your head away from me." He looked at Ted. "You believe this guy, Teddy? Who's gonna cuff him, you?"

"Where's the gun, Speedy Gonzales?" Teddy asked Kal.

Kal took deep breaths, and ignored Teddy's question.

"Come on, Kal. Don't play dumb. The one you were just using to shoot bullets at us with."

The rich boy gave no sign that he had ever used, saw or knew about a gun.

Teddy aimed his gun at Kal's right eye. "Where's the gun, fuckhead?"

Kal pointed to the lot that they had just run through.

"Okay, Jackie. I'll stay with speedy here. You go back and get the gun."

Jackie mumbled, "With my luck it'll be in a pile of dog shit," and walked toward the vacant lot. While he was on his way, Teddy put the cuffs on Kal and read him his rights. Then he and Kal walked up the street to join Jackie.

"I don't see it, Ted." Jackie sounded frustrated as hell.

"Fuckin' asshole," Jackie turned to Kal, "What'd you do with the gun?

As if Ted had not just asked him a question, as if Jackie was not searching the disgusting, trash-strewn lot, and as if they weren't standing there ready to kill him if he didn't get an answer fast....

"Do I need to call a lawyer?" Kal asked.

Teddy looked at Kal as if he were trying to decide whether to shoot him or strangle him. His fantasy was broken when Jackie came up to the car with an object wrapped in a plastic bag.

"That it, Jackie?"

"Yep."

"Where was it?"

Jackie grimaced as he walked toward the back of the car. "You don't wanna know. Open the trunk."

Kal wanted to make a call, and knew from being a fan of one of television's most popular shows, "Law and Order," that it was his right.

If he were a parolee, a drug addict, poor, or anyone with significant pigment no matter what class, Sal might have fucked with him a little before giving him access to the phone. In this case he didn't have the option, not if he wanted to keep his job.

As soon as he told the captain that Kal was in custody he was given a quick lesson in PR. "The guys did good, Sal. The fact that the Kessler kid shot at them is a real plus. The fact that he missed is less than optimal politically, but, hey that's showbiz. I use the word showbiz in a literal sense, because from here on in that's what we're looking at." The captain stopped talking but Sallie had a feeling he had more to say. He was right. "In the paper the kid looked like a movie star. You say his sister's good looking too."

"Yes, sir."

"Thin?"

"Yeah."

"Shit. That means she's probably photogenic, Sal."

"She's pretty good looking."

"Young, rich, photogenic, fucked up, I hate that. They got everything going for them."

"How would you like me to proceed on this, captain?"

"Beat them with ugly sticks."

22

As he's channel surfing, Vooko catches a glimpse of Kal Kessler on the television screen. It 's a full-face still photo, the kind that the producers throw up onto the screen when they don't have live action footage to hold your attention. The news anchor says the young man was busted after a high-speed chase and is now in the hands of the police.

Vooko can accept the fact that the little motherfucker on the screen is the one and same dipshit who tried to snuff him out with the Lincoln. What Vooko cannot comprehend though, is the motivation behind it. It isn't as if he had violated the boy's fine-ass sister, and disgraced the family name. That sort of thing he would have no problem with: then, it would have been Kal's duty to take him out. Not being able to reach a satisfactory answer, he says to himself "Remember, you're an American now, you want to fig-ure out why he wanted you dead, maybe you better start thinking like an American."

It isn't easy. He's not rich. He doesn't have a dime for a sister, a playa for a father, a classic ride and a slammin' crib in the country, but he closes his eyes, puts his head down on the couch and tries to go there. He lets his imagination run wild 'til he gets himself inside Kal's head.

Okay he's there, he's Kal Kessler, an American, and he owns the fuck-ing world. Now he's outside the Kiki club, high as a motherfucker, and like an American, he feels he's entitled to go ahead and do whatever the fuck he wants to do. He goes to the door and asks this tall, handsome foreigner in charge of the door to let him in. The gentleman politely says no and keeps him out. Meanwhile some ass- wipe who looks like all the preppie scumbags who made his high school life a fuckin' misery goes strollin' in. Okay, he feels dissed, humiliated, lower than shit on the sidewalk. So he freaks and starts beating on the foreign club security guy, who then subdues him. Okay, but what then? Wait a week and run the man down? Un-uh, that don't play.

Fed up with his failure to comprehend why Kal would try to kill him, and determined not to give the man another chance, Vooko takes a mental journey to the land where Humpty Dumpty was pushed, that place his beloved Pashko had described, where nothing happens by accident, and lightning can strike twice in the same spot. How is he gonna keep that whack Kessler kid from ever doing him like that again?

Okay. Okay. "Vooko, Vooko," Pashko is speaking to him from the grave. "In this country" he says, " they say 'the best defense is an offense' by which they mean, kill your enemy before he kills you. Really, it is similar to our traditional way of thinking."

Vooko considers this. The logic of his deceased cousin's words is undeniable. Try as he might, he cannot recall one instance when a dead person has come from the afterlife to kill a living enemy, except in fairy tales, and this here was no fairy tale.

23

Sallie peered through the two-way mirror at a medicated, slow moving, cranky-looking Kal Kessler and his ever-upbeat attorney, Smiling Simon Kay.

Perhaps the young man would have seemed more on the happy tip if Smiling had reminded him how lucky he was to get to spend the night in his apartment alone as opposed to being somebody's bitch at Rikers. Or maybe not. You never know with a metrosexual like the young Kal Kessler. Since his arrest, Kal had showered, shaved, put on some Hugo Boss threads and Bruno Magli shoes-just like OJ…great minds etc.

Both attorney and client were equally well-tailored for a Thursday evening meet, especially considering the circumstances. In fact, they made a nice juxtaposition with Simon representing Sutton Place conservative, in his lawyerly Paul Stuart navy suit, pink body, white color cotton dress shirt, Fendi tie and Gucci loafers, and Kal sporting just what a downtown, parentally indulged, Barney's- clad criminal/artist/hipster puts on for his own murder interrogation at a local precinct.

Rubbing his hands in anticipation, Black Sallie Blue Eyes entered the room and began with his usual shtick. "Would either of you like something to drink?" Simon Kay, to his credit, said he'd take whatever was on offer. Kal was mute on the subject.

"Kal, do you mind if I call you Kal, or would you like me to refer to you as Mr. Kessler."

Smiling Simon spoke for him with a hint of his renowned levity, "I think it would be safe to call him by his first name, detective. His father is Mr. Kessler."

"Okay, Kal, you can call me Sal. Hey, that rhymes. Funny, don't you think?" Kal gave him a weak, dismissive, royal nod. "So Kal, do you have any idea why you're here?" the detective seated himself and scratched the back of his neck, while observing his medicated detainee.

"No."

Sallie glanced at Simon Kay and from the tight look on his face and his client's brief answer surmised the attorney had counseled Kal to say as little as possible. "You shot at two policemen today."

Before Kal could begin, Kay reminded his client, "A yes or no will do, Kal."

"I was high and scared. I didn't know what I was doing," Kal blurted. Rebel without a pause. Kal was obviously not taking his lawyer's good advice to heart.

"We found a car in your parents' garage that was used in a hit and run." Sallie surreptitiously watched as Kal's eyes widened and then focused on his manicured fingernails. During the long ensuing silence, Sallie checked out his own fingernails. They were completely bitten down, offering up nothing for the rough edge of the emery board to file. "Your prints were found inside the vehicle," he pressed on. "How do you explain that?"

Kal shrugged. "Donny let me borrow it every once in a while."

"Had you ever gotten into an accident with it?"

"No."

"How do you explain the dents and broken mirror on the driver's side?"

"It was like that when I got it."

Sallie pinched the bridge of his nose and talked into the palm of his hand. "Tell me about the night you tried to get into the Kiki Club to see your sister. We talked about it in your apartment a couple days ago."

"You've said enough, Kal," Kay instructed his client.

Kal cut him off at the pass with a lugubrious smile. "Let me handle this, Simon."

Sal kept his game face on with great effort. He was loving the budding acrimony he sensed between client and attorney.

"I never was inside the club."

"Do you remember the bouncer?"

"Which one?"

"The one you decked pretty good before you were restrained." Again young Kessler's lawyer intervened.

Sal overrode it with, "Look, counselor, I'm trying to figure out how it was that the bouncer who subdued your client wound up getting hit by the exact type car that has your client's fingerprints all over it."

"He already said that it wasn't his car."

Again, Sal ignored the attorney and eyed Kal. "We have testimony from the Kiki bouncer that you were the driver of the vehicle that ran him down. By the way, do you know anyone named Scholar?"

"No," cavalierly stated.

"He's someone who lives in the Frederick Douglass housing projects." Sallie said. "Anything else you'd like to share with Mr. Kay and me about Scholar, Kal?"

"That's about it. What else do you want me to say?"

"I was hoping you would ask me that," Sal said, "because I don't think you've given your attorney a clear understanding of who Scholar is and what your relationship is to him." He opened a folder and handed Scholar's rap sheet to the attorney. "I'm going to try again, Kal. Is there anything else you want to say regarding Scholar? I hear you two have been busy partying in the Hamptons."

Kal turned red. He scanned the room as if looking for a rock to crawl under. His lips remained tightly closed.

Sal tapped his fingertips on the table. "Your friend Scholar said you purchased a gun and shot and killed a man the same night you ran down his cousin Vooko."

For one small piece of a moment Kal opened his lips to say something, but his attorney covered them with his hand. "Don't say a fucking thing, Kal!"

Throughout his career, Sallie had accumulated some wonderful memories of witness interrogations. Watching how quickly Simon Kay had snapped at his client was one for the collection.

Before their arrival, Sallie had ordered snacks for all of them. He took this opportunity to signal for them to be brought in. An officer carried a tray and placed it in the center of the table. "Help yourself," he said. "Go, take something. We may be here a while." And just to fuck with Kay, he added in his most polite manner, "The bagels are made around the corner. They're fresh, soft, really good, maybe the best in the city. You like bagels, Simon?"

"Thanks," Kay said, selecting a poppy-seed one. He pushed the tray toward Kal. "Eat something. You'll feel better," he said.

Sallie seemed so relaxed and at ease, he might have been hosting a backyard picnic for three. The other two didn't radiate the same sense of enjoyment, just the opposite in fact. Simon Kay, whose trade required anticipating when the other shoe would drop, looked anxiously at the detective. History had taught him that disastrous information often came in sums greater than one and the recent information about Scholar meant one was down, and he hoped it wasn't going to be two to go. Kal Kessler took mouse bites of his sandwich, looking, due to the high amount of prescription downers Sallie guessed he'd ingested, considerably less apprehensive than his lawyer.

"Counselor," Sallie said. "I don't want to ruin your meal, but let me tell you something. Before he was arrested, Kal threw a gun in a pile of fresh dog shit, which my young associate practically slipped on while retrieving the evidence." Sallie paused to make sure the image registered. "The gun was the same type used to kill the security guy from the club. We're having Ballistics check it out to see if it was the murder weapon."

"Christ!" the veteran criminal attorney said, shooting some of his half chewed sandwich out of his mouth and across the table. Sallie used a folder to swipe the pieces to the floor.

"I didn't shoot anyone!" Kal said, tossing his half-eaten bagel onto the tray.

"Don't say one more fucking thing!" Simon Kay interjected, and this time it sounded like he'd *really* meant it.

24

The hitmaker was behind the console. "Sorry to bother you at this time of day, Biz," Jackie said, eyeing the engineer after giving a nod to the producer. "Could we have a few minute's privacy?"

"No problem," Biz said.

As they seated themselves in the comfortable captain's chairs, Jackie removed a small writing pad from his shirt pocket. "I won't waste your time or mine with needless chitchat, my brother. You know we're doing a murder investigation. I have a few questions that need answers. What did you charge to produce that joint for Scholar?"

"Fifteen large."

"Is that your usual fee?"

"I usually don't do demos. But that was the number I gave Scholar, because I had to say somethin'. The man was all the time buggin' me. He kept sayin', 'Yo, Little Man, when we gonna get down?'" Biz laughed at his own imitation of Scholar. "So I came up with what I thought was a ridiculous number."

"Thinking he'd never get it?"

"Word."

"But he got it." Jackie confirmed, as he wrote the figure in his notebook.

Biz nodded. "He did. Two payments. Ten the first time, and five the second time."

"When was this?"

"The first one was a week ago Monday or Tuesday night before the recording session, and the other was Thursday night, at the start of it."

"Did he say where he got the money at?"

"He didn't say and I didn't ask."

"Why do you think he came to you to produce his joint?"

"Where else was he gonna go? He doesn't know anybody."

"Were you surprised when he came up with the money?"

"Man, before he even asked me would I do it, he put a wad of cash in front of me. Was I surprised? I nearly fell out the chair."

"Where did this happen."

"Some studio over in Times Square."

"What were you doing there?"

"Mixing a joint for this white boy over at Atlantic Records."

Jackie kept on. "So one minute you're sitting at a board like the one in front of us, and the next minute, Scholar comes in and throws money on it?"

Biz grinned. "Am I Biz or what?"

"I hear that!" Jackie smacked him a five. "Was he excited? Chill? What was his mood like?"

"Man, to tell you the truth, he seemed out of his head. He's hyper all the time anyway. This was ODB fucked up. The dude was scaring me."

Jackie glanced up from his book, where he had been scribbling notes. "ODB from the Wu? He was that high?"

"If he wasn't, he's a bigger psycho than I imagined. And believe me man, I got a good imagination."

"Was he alone when he came in?"

"Word."

"Next time you saw him was...let's see..." Jackie referred to his notes. "Thursday. You were producing Proof Positive. Friday, you played it in person for Sunn. Last Saturday night, you saw him and Proof do Ray at the Kiki. Right? You heard from him since?"

Biz clamped his eyes shut like he was ordered not to peek. "Once more...before y'all arrested him again. He came over to this studio and started giving me some bullshit about how I hadn't lived up to our agreement and I had to get back into the studio with Proof."

"Proof Positive? Did you?"

"Hell, no. Didn't have time. You locked up their asses the next day." Biz cracked his knuckles.

Jackie winced. He hated when people did that. "Had Scholar ever asked you to produce anything for him before?"

"Many times."

"Had he ever offered you money before?"

"You kidding? Man probably has the first nickel he stole."

"So where do you think he got the money? Fifteen G is a whole lot of cheddar."

"Word. How would I know?"

Jackie tucked his notebook back into his shirt pocket. "What do you think of Ray? Is he for real?"

"Straight up."

"And Scholar?"

"I might trust him to dead someone, if there was money in it. Know what I'm sayin'?"

"That's exactly what I've been thinking. Thanks for your time."

Sallie was at his desk when Jackie returned from seeing Biz. "Hey, Gleason, what have you got for me? I just sent Ted up to Mamaroneck to get the details on the Donovan case. I would have gone myself, but the captain ordered me to stay here to field questions. The media is all over both of these cases. I've never been involved before in anything so many folks want to know about."

Jackie slid onto the chair opposite Sal's. "Check this out, boss. A few days before Pashko was killed, Scholar paid Biz fifteen large. Where does a mook like that come up with that kinda green?"

"I don't have a clue, Jackie, but I bet you're gonna tell me."

"Try this. Imagine you're a violent young psycho."

"I was," Sallie laughed at the memory.

Jackie laughed with him. "Okay. Scholar wants to make a demo with his group. It costs money, lots of it. He knows Kal is a limitless ATM, because he's been supplying him with drugs. Kal tells Scholar about the incident at the club from his point of view, which is how this big guy dissed him in front of his sister, etc. Scholar tells him he can take care of it...for a price."

"Sounds plausible." Sallie closed his eyes and imagined the scene at the Kiki. "Scholar and Kal make some kind of deal. Scholar goes to the club at closing that night. He waits for Vooko. Instead, he sees *two* guys who look like the one he's supposed to whack. He panics and shoots at both of them. He manages to get one of them, but the other runs away. And here's where our John-the-car-thief's story comes into play. While Pashko is having a bullet fired point blank into his head, courtesy of Scholar, Vooko runs over to Fifth Avenue to escape."

Sallie shot straight up in his chair. His hands were trembling from excitement. "What if Kal is up the block watching this whole thing go down? He sees Vooko running away. He follows him, catches up to him, and hits him with the Navigator."

Jackie grinned. "That's good, Sallie. I like that. Now what is Kessler doing in Donny's car?"

"That I don't know. But remember, Donny has many cars. He could have loaned the Navigator to Kal. Maybe Kal was smart enough to know his Aston would be easy to identify."

"What has Forensics said about the damage to the Navigator?"

Sallie tapped a folder on his desk. "The dents are consistent with what would happen if the driver had hit a very large individual."

"Are there any fibers we can match to Vooko's clothes?"

"The lab report said it's a little early to tell."

As he waited for the blue-eyed barney fife, Scholar thought about his fucked up predicament. No matter which direction he went, the road led to a place he didn't want to go—a bleak upstate penitentiary, where he'd freeze his ass off in winter and get bitten to death by roach-sized mosquitoes in the suffocating heat of the summer.

The thought was more than depressing. He'd gotten a taste of the good life and he was feeling it, too. That weekend with Kal at Golden Pond Farm opened him up, yo. Kal's joint made those hip-hop houses on "Cribs" look like Uncle Tom's cabin. He could sum it up in one word— class. *Man, all them suckers who thought they was hot shit with all their big-ass entertainment rooms and pimp- ass furniture...they had no idea what the word 'class' meant.* He thought about the polished silver candelabra over the grand piano, paintings by Picasso yo, original, not some shabby-ass museum copy, oriental rugs, not wool, my brothers, but silk, and how 'bout them double thick cotton bed sheets and plush-ass towels?

Scholar threw himself onto his lumpy mattress and stared at the wall. He remembered telling the Proof all about his weekend in the Hamptons. "Livin' the lifestyle of the rich and famous is like livin' in heaven," he'd said. "If all goes well, that can be us in the Hamptons, yo, indoor pools, pimped-out rides, and shorties for days. Guess who might be livin' next door, yo? That fillim director David Spielberg, know what I'm sayin'? I seen him walking around this big-ass golf course they got out there. I seen Russell Simmons out there too. Motherfucker was having hisself a cappuccino with this fine-ass white bitch from the tv or some shit. For real, dawgs, I'm feelin' it." If the Proof felt it too, they weren't letting on, *motherfuckin' peasants.*

Now, here he was, in jail and feeling sorry for himself. If he'd known about it earlier, he might've learned geogrammy or whatever, to move up the ladder and get his hands on some of the good life. The Kessler house had shown him what an ignorant peasant he was. Made him feel less than human. *Damn.* He wished he'd never met Kal. Never dreamed his stupid hip-hop dreams. Pea Head, Science, and that Judas, Freeze...*Man, they's nothin'. I'm nothin'. Life is a worldwide conspiracy to fuck a brotha up and keep him down.*

"Hey, Scholar, how're you doin', buddy?"

Scholar rolled over on to eyeball the speaker. There he was, the blue-eyed man, tryin' to get inside his head again. "Yo, man. Survivin' is thrivin'." He sauntered over to the bars.

Sallie nodded. "That's good to hear. Listen, I need to ask a few more questions, if you don't mind."

"It's all good."

"You said that boy Kal shot the guy at the Kiki last Saturday. Right?"

"Wrong. I say he buy a gat."

"That's right. Who'd he buy it from? You have any idea?"

"Man, how'm I gonna know a thing like that?"

"I won't know if I don't ask, and you seem to know quite a bit."

"Word. I do get around."

"By the way, where'd you get the money to pay for that demo you played for Sunn?"

"What you mean?"

"You went up to Sunn's to play a demo. Who produced it?"

Scholar stretched his arms above his head. All of a sudden, the man with the questions seemed to have the answers, too. He could feel the walls of his cage closin' in on him. "I produced it myself."

"I thought you were a manager."

"I am. But I'm a producer also."

"You know a guy named Biz?"

"Who?"

"Scholar, he's your cousin. Remember what I said about rhetorical questions? That was one of them."

"Since you know the answers, why don't you tell me 'bout Biz?"

"You paid him fifteen thousand dollars to produce that demo. Where'd you get that kind of cash?"

"I want myself a lawyer, yo."

"No problem. We'll get you one…soon."

"I want one now, detective."

"In a minute. I want to get a few things straight."

"Don't see how I can help you."

"I think you got that money from Kal, Scholar. I think he paid you to shoot someone, but you shot the wrong guy."

"I don't know nothin' about no shootin'."

"Well, let me leave you with this thought. Not only did you shoot the guy, but after you shot him, you gave the gun to Kal."

"Said I didn't shoot nobody."

"Okay. Have it your way. I'll be around."

25

Vooko picked up a copy of the News and headed down to the diner. His favorite booth, the one in the far corner that overlooked the street, was empty. He sat down, made himself comfortable and opened the paper. Amazing. At least five full pages of people he knew. On the top of page three, he saw the dickhead who had run him over, as well as the beautiful shorty who hit him upside the head with a shoe. The story starting just below their movie star faces described them as the privileged children of real estate mogul Sheldon Kessler. Vooko looked at the picture of the middle-aged tycoon, and Donny Donovan, the lawyer his friend Bobby Sanchez was buddies with. He was dead. Damn, the world was getting more dangerous by the second! And fuck! There, next to the picture of Donny and Bobby, was none other than his boss, Neil Weinstein, looking stressed and old standing in front of the Kiki Club. Neil. Too bad, Neil was a good guy.

Suddenly, Vooko felt like someone had knocked the wind out of him. There, in black and white, was a large picture of him and Pashko! The good memory it evoked made him so sad. Pashko had come outside the club to see how Vooko was doing at his new job. He was happy and Pashko was beaming with pride, because his cuz had been able to get him a job, yo! Bobby had snapped it of the two of them at a beautiful moment. How good was that? Pashko's positive charge jumped out of the page in the paper, took Vooko's heart and caused it to race. Buckets of tears fell from his eyes onto the black and white pages. It was tragic, monumentally fuckin' tragic.

WHO DO YOU BELIEVE? That was the headline of the next story he looked at. Below it was another picture of Kal Kessler and a separate one of Scholar, who the paper identified as the manager of a hip-hop group called Proof Positive. Vooko couldn't help but notice how Kal's picture looked more like a poster boy in an ad from GQ and Scholar's like one from America's Most Wanted. Vooko felt himself grinding his teeth. The fuckin' media always makin' it so the rich folks look good.

The article was whack, made no sense. The writer presented Kal as an innocent man who was in the wrong place at the wrong time, and the scowling man with the prison tats as a convicted felon who "is suspected in the murderer of the hard working immigrant, Pashko Gazivoda, outside the Kiki Club in Manhattan last week."

Tears hovered in Vooko's eyes, but he continued to read. The article reported that Kal Kessler was out on bail while his accuser, Scholar, was being held for other violent offenses. Reading faster, Vooko noticed there was no mention of Kal being investigated for a hit and run.

By the time his chicken parmesan platter arrived, he had finished reading yet another article. This one was accompanied by a big-ass house with a Kessler Estate, East Hampton sign in front. It described how angry the owner Sheldon Kessler was at the NYPD for associating his son with murder. He intended to sue the city, unless apologies were given for the outrage. He had special hostility toward Detective Salvatore Messina. The cop's picture was there, too, his eyes cold as ice, coming out of the page like laser lights, yo, comin' right at Vooko, penetrating his brain. That was one edgy looking motherfucker.

The story about the detective said he was a highly decorated cop who had a successful history of working undercover jobs for the department. It went on about his heroics in a hostage situation that had made the news five years ago. Some nut was on a shooting rampage in a Soho boutique, where Messina was shopping with his wife. According to a witness, Messina "announced he was with the NYPD, which was when the guy took a hostage. Everything happened fast after that. Shots were exchanged, and, in a matter of seconds, the hostage was freed and the gunman was on the ground in handcuffs." The writer called Messina a true New York hero.

Vooko had been so involved in reading the article that he'd failed to read it's headline KESSLER TAKES AIM AT HERO DETECTIVE.

Sallie chose a table in the back at the always welcoming Molly's She-been, and ordered a dark Guinness and shepherd's pie. He needed time alone and some sustenance to collect his thoughts. No one would bother him back here. The relentlessness of the investigation was finally getting to him. He had everyone crawling over him, including the captain, Neil, the mayor, Kessler and his attorneys, and the entire press for answers and they all wanted to have them now.

With his drink situated nicely next to his steaming pie, he went over the case again, hoping the evidence he had would lead him to something conclusive. At this point Vooko's testimony placed Kal at the Kiki scene. The damage to Donny's car was helpful for the hit and run and Kal's finger-prints were in it, but it still didn't connect Kal to Pashko's murder. Freeze said Scholar did that job, but Scholar denied it. And then there was the gun. Although they'd caught Kal in possession of the gun that ballistics identified as the same one used to fire the bullets into Pashko, he simply couldn't believe Kal was the shooter. If Kal had really been in the Naviga-tor, he would have been too busy running Vooko down to have had time to shoot Pashko. And Donny. Who the hell had shot Donny and why?

26

Two o'clock in the morning. She was up and would be happy to meet him in her neighborhood. Sal asked where? She picked the Empire Diner. Same place he used to brunch with ex number two. Hey, whatever made Lady Panther happy. The art deco diner on Tenth Avenue had good food, good service and it was quiet enough to carry on a conversation. It also had the benefit of being a place where a person could talk about every sort of sexual predilection without raising an eyebrow. With its proximity to kinky afterhours clubs, and the meat packing district, named for its butchers and meat-packing hard core leather boy night life a few blocks away, this part of the city was no stranger to freak shows.

Sal thought she looked good on her website, but Lady's star quality presence in the flesh overwhelmed him. He observed with some humor, how she made him feel conspicuously unworthy of her company. "Hello, detective. It's good to meet you." Her handshake was firm and warm. "Thanks for coming alone. You're partner's a goon."

Sal skipped over the reference to Ted and unexpectedly found himself saying something very old fashioned and— worse, almost goofy. "You're more beautiful than your pictures."

Shana blushed. "You're sort of cute yourself."

"Thank you."

"No it's nothing. Thank you, detective."

Sallie led her to an empty booth.

"Shana, or would you prefer that I call you something else," he gushed.

"Shana is good."

"Would you like something to drink?"

"Some water would be nice. I'm always watching my weight."

When the pale waiter in the black Radio Head tee shirt and black Converse high-tops casually came over to take their order Sal said "Water for her and an iced tea for me, please."

Sallie, feeling suddenly self-conscious, shifted uncomfortably in his side of the booth. "As I explained, this is a murder investigation. I think Teddy spoke to you about Pashko. We know who killed him, and we believe we know why. So that's pretty wrapped up. It's Donny Donovan I need to know more about."

She paused a moment, and took a breath, "When I saw the story of him in the paper, it freaked me right out."

"I can imagine having two clients murdered one after the other would have that effect."

Their drinks arrived.

"Did Donny know Pashko?"

"Not that I know of."

"We know how Pashko came to you. How did Donny?"

"I have a friend who is sort of a bodybuilding superstar. She introduced me to him."

"How did she know Donny?"

"He was a client. Body worship. Ya know, paid to rub oil on her muscles, massage her, stuff like that. No sex or wrestling, not with her."

"What did she say about him?"

"Not much, really. Just that he paid and I had nothing to worry about."

"Does she refer many clients to you?"

"Once in a while."

"Once in a while can mean many things."

"You're right. I see, detective. Maybe three in two years."

"Where did you and Donny meet?"

"The first few times we met up at his place in Westchester. He'd send a limo for me. Very considerate."

"Then what happened?"

"I'd let him put some oil on me. Then we'd wrestle."

"Who won?"

"He did."

"He did? Did you let him?"

"No. He had size on me and he was in great shape. He was very competitive. I don't think he's used to losing."

The two of them sat in silence. Sallie kept his eyes on her face. She blushed.

"Stop that. You're looking at me like I'm a criminal."

"Sorry. I know you're not a criminal."

"So, stop okay?"

"Okay." Sallie sighed while he turned to look out the window to the all night gas station across the street. "So, what happened next?"

"Well he told me he was going to change the venue. A friend of his had a gym set up and wanted to watch."

"Did he tell you about the friend?"

"I didn't ask and he didn't say anything more. I deal in confidentiality. You understand."

"So now you're at the gym? The one his friend has."

"Right. First, me and Donny wrestled alone. Nobody else was there, which I thought was odd since I sort of expected to see his friend."

"Okay." The conversation was flowing, like effortless dancing.

"Then about halfway into it his friend came in."

"And then."

"His friend watched for a while, and then Donny asked me to take a seat."

"There were chairs there?"

"A couple. Black leather, very luxurious."

"Then what?"

"He and Donny wrestled."

"Just the two of them? While you watched?" She nodded and took a sip of her water.

"Okay," Sal pressed on, "You're watching these two guys go at it. What was that like?"

"Very intense, like gladiators in ancient Rome"

"What did his friend look like?"

"Hard to say."

"He wore a mask? Did you think that was odd?"

"Not really, no."

Sallie put both palms in front of his eyes and rubbed. After he lowered them, he took a sip of tea. "What kind of mask, Shana?"

"A leather one. It was a leather one, standard s and m issue."

"Full face?"

"Yeah."

"How about his body, was that covered too."

"He wore shorts and tight fitting top, high leather shoes. The guy was in great shape."

"Could you recognize him if you saw him?"

"No way."

"Who won?"

"I would say they were evenly matched despite the size difference. The other guy was quick and he knew what he was doing."

"Did anybody else ever show up?"

"Once. The man came in with a woman."

"With a woman?"

"But I never saw her face. Yeah, she was wearing a mask too. It mostly covered her eyes and forehead."

"What sort of clothes did she have on?"

"Sweat pants, sneakers, a raincoat and a scarf over her head. Expensive. Designer stuff. I think the shoes were Prada."

"What did she do there?"

"She sat on a chair near me."

"While the men wrestled?"

"Yes."

"How long did the woman stay for?"

"Maybe a minute."

"Did she ever see you wrestle with Donny?"

"No."

"Did you ever wrestle Donny's friend?"

"No."

"Have you heard from Donny's friend since Donny died."

"No."

They sat in silence. She was fiddling with her glass. Sallie was thinking that what she had to say was credible. It fit with his theory."

"So is that it detective?"

"Yeah, Shana, I think that's it."

"You ever try wrestling, detective?" she had a wonderful smile and her eyes seemed to look right through him.

"You know, Shana, I can honestly say, with women, only the psychological kind."

She laughed, then gazed at him intently, "Would you like to try?"

Sallie turned crimson. "As in try with you?"

"Was there somebody else you had in mind?"

"You know I never really thought about it. Basketball is my sport."

"Oh, yeah? Where do you play?"

"Down the street over at the Piers."

"I'd like to see that."

"You would?"

"I like you, detective. Cute guys with brains, manners and steady employment are a rarity in this town."

"Thanks, I'll take that as a compliment."

"Well, keep it in mind."

With that she put ten dollars on the counter and left.

27

Kal rushed out of his apartment building and ran across the street to the parking ramp where he kept his two cars. He needed some air, some space, and some drugs. And he wasn't about to head out all the way to Rockaway to get them either. Minutes later, he and his Z4 roadster were blasting up the West Side Highway. The sky was clear, but his head was far from it. Fuck his father. Yeah, the old man was furious with him. He'd paid big bucks to get his son out on bail, but that seemed to be as far as he would go to support him. His fucking father had actually said, "A little time in prison might do you some good. Teach you to appreciate all I've given you." Then he'd gotten up in Kal's face, shoved him away and added, "You're such a fuck up. What the hell were you doing waving that murder weapon at the police?"

The prescription sedatives he'd been taking made him feel low. And now he needed to get high. He pulled off the highway in Washington Heights and moved down Broadway. Somewhere around 155th Street, he headed west toward the river. This was the neighborhood where he used to score back in the days when New York was still scary. When there was no such thing as a neighborhood you could feel safe in because bad shit happened everywhere. It was fun then, had a nice edge to it. Now, because of guys like his father, the city was a eunuch, a Disneyland version of its former balls-to-the wall self. Thankfully, this part of Manhattan had been spared. He drove past the same shabby apartment buildings he remembered from years ago. The street reeked of urine, and garbage was piled up everywhere. It was just like old times.

In under three minutes, he had the drugs in his trembling hands. Within the next two he had moved his ride to a nearby corner where he parked, and rapid fire torched his new shopping presents. As the smoke filled his lungs, he felt resurrected. With "Licensed to Ill" raging on his car stereo, he screamed onto the FDR. For a while everything was flowing nicely. Just a while though, then some driver in a maroon, piece-of-shit car in front of him put on his brakes and practically came to a stop.

Kal pulled around it. "Fucking asshole," he screamed, flipping the guy the bird.

As he did, the driver flashed his lights and waved. What the fuck was that all about? Kal took another look, this time from his rearview mirror. The guy behind the wheel was pointing a gun at him and seemed to be saying bang, bang. Kal sped up. So did the little car. Kal heard shots. He floored it. There was no traffic in the near distance and he kicked the Beemer into overdrive, hoping to make the little car disappear. He kept going faster and faster. At One Hundred Tenth Street he was doing a Hundred Ten MPH. But he was going too fast to take note of the ironic coincidence.

The tweaker was tearing the highway up. The city was flying by. Around Ninety-Sixth Street two cars with Jersey plates, and kids driving, pulled to the right and left of him. He put the pedal to the metal, and the car responded with a jolt. The Jersey delinquents sped up too. What the fuck is this? Kal thought, the Garden State Parkway? Do I know these guys? In fact he didn't. They were just a couple of bridge and tunnel idiots come to the big city to race each other to the end of the highway. By the time they had reached the Seventy-Second Street exit all three cars were running neck and neck. Maybe it was the excellent cocktail of smoke and fear, but the faster Kal went, the slower it felt; he kept desperately stepping on the gas pedal to try to go faster.

Somewhere around Sixty-Eighth Street a terrible thought dawned on him. The guy with the gun in the maroon car was the guy from Kiki, the guy he had run over with Donny's car while Scholar gunned down his identical twin cousin, instead of him.

The light they were coming up to at Fifty-Ninth Street was changing from yellow to red. The Jersey cars saw it and stepped on their brakes. Kal was not going to stop. Not with that maniac with the gun behind him.

As he got closer to the intersection, he saw a garbage truck pulling into the lot west of the highway. Kal felt for sure that, if he kept going, he could squeeze by it, which he was able to do. If he had had the time, he would have celebrated, but he didn't. Yes, he had successfully avoided colliding with the massive white behemoth he saw, but he was less successful in avoiding the one behind it that he didn't see.

John Gotti is known to have said, "The one that gets you, you never see it coming." The collision was fast and furious; a case in point that drugs and driving don't mix. The outcome was predictable. How could a prissy little BMW sports car plow into ten tons of steel loaded with five tons of garbage and remain intact? The answer: it couldn't, and neither could its driver.

With his height advantage, Vooko had an unobstructed view of the people on the ramp getting out of their cars to see what happened. He was in a state of emotional confusion. Death was so final, and he wasn't sure that the messy outcome was the way he wanted it to end. In a way all he had wanted to do was fuck with Kal's head for a while. That's why he followed him from his house to the Heights, and from there Southbound on the highway where he showed him his gun, bang bang. That had definitely scared the little fucker.

"Well what's done is done," he thought. "Too bad." He drove around the block and headed back uptown.

Thirty minutes later, Sallie was surveying the accident scene. The police pushed back the curious gawkers to make room for three EMT ambulances and several patrol cars. Kal was the only casualty. The guys in the big truck were a little shaky but they were going to be all right. Someone had already gotten word out to the press. TV crews from every network and cable show were there, as well as photographers from the local papers. No doubt the violent death would sell millions of copies, especially because the victim was a good-looking rich kid with a famous father. Sal could practically see the headlines now: ANGEL? DEVIL? KAL, WE HARDLY KNEW YOU. Under the caption would be a half page picture of the pretty boy in his best suit.

Sheldon Kessler had arrived too, and had quickly tried to move beyond the barricades. When he saw Sallie, he bum rushed him. The detective didn't move away fast enough and caught a fist on the ear. "You're responsible for this, Messina!" Sheldon screamed, as he threw some body blows. In seconds, a group of officers were all over him. Kessler kicked and screamed until he realized what he was up against and then stood looking angry and bewildered. Sallie remained composed. "Let him go," he said.

The officers did as he asked. Sheldon Kessler stood for a moment facing Sallie in the dim light of approaching dusk. "I'm sorry for your loss," Sallie said, aware that the cameras were rolling. "This isn't over! *This isn't over*, Messina! Not by a long shot!" Kessler growled.

28

Obsessed, obsessed and obsessed, and holding on to every detail, Sallie stared at the ceiling of his small bedroom. It was two a.m. and he was too jacked on adrenaline to sleep. The pieces of the puzzle were beginning to form a picture, just how he liked it. It was coming slowly, but it was coming. He put on his sweats, walked west to the Hudson and ran south along the river a good couple of miles until his endorphins were ripping, then he ran back. A nice calm was on him now. By four thirty, he was home in the same position as before, on his bed, face up to the ceiling. With his mind full of facts, he went into a half sleep, knowing that, in this relaxed state, subconscious would make its own connections until the inevitable magic moment of his epiphany, the point where the when, the how, and the why behind the fact that Pashko and Donny were no longer among the living would be concisely and logically laid out before him with the precision of an algebraic equation.

When it came he stepped onto his cold-to-the-touch, hardwood floor, and headed for the shower. Minutes later, he was on his way to the neighborhood bakery where he ordered a large latte, and sat at a marble table as it was being made. A television set, mounted on the wall in front of him, was tuned to New York One, the twenty-four hour local news station. The announcer gave the weather forecast and the traffic update. By then, Sallie was sipping his coffee and getting ready to butter a hot croissant. When he glanced at the screen, he saw a coiffed young man, microphone in hand, wind blowing his hair in that perfect action reporter way, describing the chase that lead to the death of Kal Kessler and then concluded with "Kal was the only son of Sheldon Kessler, a well-known New York real estate developer."

Behind the announcer, the bright lights of emergency vehicles were flashing color on the scene, as the same strong off-the-river wind that was giving him his action look, lifted newspapers and plastic bags into the air. The camera swept over the metal carnage that was once a BMW and city garbage truck. The atmosphere was exactly the way Sallie remembered it—frenetic, edgy, and terminal.

The next shot showed a manic Kessler attacking a calm man in a jacket and tie. The man was Sal professionally deflecting the barrage of blows, followed by Sal again this time telling the police to release the man, who by then they had restrained—but not before the camera caught Kessler's face as his ferociously demented voice wailed : "This isn't over, Messina!"

That piece of drama would likely serve Sal well. For now though, it was far from over. Days ago Sheldon had crossed the line and now Sal had an obligation to see that he be held accountable.

Sallie had a second croissant, then cabbed it the ten minutes from his apartment to the station. On his desk, he found a note from the captain: COME TO MY OFFICE ASAP.

"Sallie, you're killing me." The Buddha motioned for him to have a seat.

"I take it you saw the news." Sallie draped a leg over the arm of the chair.

"Along with half of New York, including the mayor, and all of Police Plaza." The Buddha scratched his head and rubbed his eyes. "The commissioner got a call from the mayor wanting to know why this department was harassing his friend Sheldon."

"Nobody's harassing Sheldon, Captain."

"That's Sheldon's position."

"Based on what?" Sallie could feel his temper rising.

"It doesn't matter what it's based on. The guy with the biggest PR firm in the city wins. You know that. I hate this kind of bullshit." The captain scrubbed his face and glared at his protégée.

"What do you want me to do?"

"Wrap it up."

"That's what I'm trying to do."

"Get it done sooner, rather than later, Sal. The longer it takes, the more time Kessler has to get his damn face in the paper. Look at it from the public's point of view. The guy is grieving. His son just suffered an untimely and horrific death. Any father would go a little crazy under such circumstances. Even I feel for him." The captain took a sip of tea. "I'm sorry he hit you. I guess he had to lash out at someone, you can understand that. Hope it didn't hurt too much." The captain gazed at Sallie sympathetically. "Okay. Enough said. You took it like a man, Sal. You get points for that. Just do what you have to do to get it done. I'll be here holding off the drama queens."

Sallie returned to his desk and dialed a 718 area code and a seven digit number. "Vooko. This is Detective Messina from the city. You don't happen to drive a maroon Toyota, by any chance?" When Vooko didn't respond, Sallie continued. "Look, I know the vehicle belonged to your cousin, Pashko. I got information that a maroon Toyota fled the scene of an accident last night. I know it was you," Sal paused, "The guy's dead. End of story, but I need to know who killed your cousin, Pashko. I need you to come down here to identify the killer. Now."

There was dead silence from Vooko's end.

Sallie was at the end of his rope. "Hey Vooko, I don't give a shit about the Molotov cocktail. No one got hurt. We can keep that between ourselves, too. " Sallie waited, but all he got was more of the same. Nothing. "I know who killed Pashko. I need you to identify him for me."

Vooko still didn't respond.

Sallie had to smile. This kid Vooko was a piece of work. "If you're thinking you might get another crack at the killer, forget it, Vooko. He's going away for a very long time and to a place that's very cold in the winter and hot as hell in the summer. You don't want to go there. I'll say it again. Kal is dead. Look, I promise you and I don't bullshit, ask Neil. You won't be held responsible for the accident that Kal died in. But, if you don't help me out here, I can't help you out, which means I'm gonna have to confiscate your car, take you in for tossing the Molotov, and all kinds of other unpleasantness that I want to avoid."

"I'll leave here in about fifteen minutes," Vooko replied.

Sallie sighed. "You want me to have Neil send a car for you?"

"No. I'll take the subway."

While Vooko was heading downtown, Sallie moved on to his next order of business. Pea Head and Science were already seated behind a table in the interrogation room. "I'm gonna make this short and, hopefully, sweet," he said, as soon as he closed the door behind him. I know what happened at the Kiki last Saturday night. You guys stomped the shit out of one of Sunn's producer and Freeze cut him."

The two members of The Proof gaped at him like he'd just showed them a magic trick. Sallie went on with his spiel, sugared with lots of compassion. "That's something I can understand, knowing your background and all. You guys worked hard. Thought you had a shot at a label deal. You felt you'd been disrespected and you wanted to vent a little rage. That's all good, but what I don't understand is why you would participate in a homicide."

"I don't know what the fuck you talkin' about, man," Pea Head said.

Science nodded. "Dat is some bullshit."

Sallie ignored their outbursts. "You guys were in a car parked on 22nd Street, near Sixth Avenue, around four- thirty in the morning."

"Na-uh, man. Don't even go there. Now you talkin' some shit." Pea Head glanced at Science, and then folded his arms over his chest.

"Word, yo." Science added. "I ain't know what you talkin' 'bout."

Sallie kept on. "All you have to do is nod like this, if I'm right." Sallie nodded then waited for about five seconds to let the guys absorb what he had just said, then moved his head ever so slightly again. Pea Head and Science followed on cue like Simon says without the words. "You were smoking weed and listening to music."

Sallie nodded. Both men looked at each other and nodded too.

"Scholar got out. Said he had some business to take care of." Sallie had their full attention. He nodded. They reciprocated. "A few minutes after Scholar got out, Freeze went out."

No nods. "Guys, I need a nod." He got two hesitant nods. "A little later, Freeze came in, and then Scholar came in and you drove off." Duplicate nods. "Now I'm gonna tell you what your buddy Freeze said happened, while you were in the car, and I have every reason to believe him." Sallie clearly had their attention. "While you were in the car, Scholar went down the street and killed a man who worked at the club."

"Shit, man. We had no idea what was goin' on." Pea Head said. "We was just chillin'."

"Are you willing to make a statement?"

"'Bout what?" Pea Head asked.

"That you saw Freeze cut the producer and that you were in Scholar's car on 22nd Street at around four-thirty the night the bouncer was shot."

"Oh that. Do it mean I can walk the fuck outta here?" Pea Head cut clean to the chase.

Science interrupted him. "Look, man, I know nothin' about nothin' dat happen when we was in Scholar's car. Dat's what I'm talkin' about."

"I'm not talking about that, gentlemen. We're talking about what Freeze did at the club."

Both of the men nodded,

Sallie took it that they had reached a consensus and business was over. He called for them to be taken from the room and instructed the weekend officer to bring in Freeze.

Heat and rage emanating from him, Freeze strolled into the room. Before seating himself, he turned the chair around and draped his arms around its back.

"Sorry for the delay, Freeze," Sallie said.

"Apology accepted, detective."

"I spoke to the DA and he said he would be willing to work with us on the slice and dice."

"That's all good."

"I need to know more about the murder that night." Sallie paused. "You know, Scholar says he didn't do it. He said Kal killed the guy at the Kiki."

"It ain't so."

"So what did happen?"

"Way I see it is, Scholar needed big money for us to get into a studio. Biz, his cousin, say he produce the joint for fifteen Gs."

That wasn't exactly the answer to his question, but life had taught Sallie that there are many ways to get to an answer. "That seems like a lot of money," Sallie said hoping to move Freeze along.

"Tolt him that, yo. Tolt him his cuz was rippin' him off. I had some peeps would do it for practically nuttin', but he alla time say he wanna do it wit Biz and only Biz, 'cause Biz got the connections."

"Then what?"

"Then we in the studio and I'm like, yo, Scholar, where you get the cheddar for this here? He's like 'that's what a manager do.'"

"How do you think he got the money?"

"Man, I don't gotta think 'bout it. I know. That white boy pay him to do the guy at Kiki."

Finally, there it was. The answer Sallie had been waiting for. Patience had paid off. "How do you know that?"

"Why else he gonna do that?"

"Drugs?"

"No, man. Look, I seen Scholar pop the bouncer dude, and you know what else? I seen that same skinny white guy, that give him the money, in a big black Navigator waitin' just up the street that night. And when Scholar do his thing, I seen the kid drive off."

"You see anything else?"

"No, man, I jus' bounced back to the car."

"There was a murder upstate, possibly done with the same gun, Freeze. You think Scholar did that one, too?"

"No way."

"Why not?"

"'Cause right after Scholar done that dude at Kiki, that crazy white boy met up wit us in Far Rock."

"Where?" Sallie put his hands up to his temples and started massaging. His mind was in high gear trying to process the new information and he felt a headache coming on.

"That parkin' lot where you picked us up that night."

"The Molotov night?"

"Say what?"

"The night of the firebomb."

"Word. Scholar, he gets outta his car, talks to that kid and comes back wit fifteen hundrit. I'm like 'Yo, Scholar, what you doin' wit all that green?' He say 'I just engage in some buy low, sell high capitalism.'"

"He said that?"

"Yeah. Those was his exact words."

"Did you ask him what he meant?"

"Didn't have to, man. He tolt me like he was Big Willy. He sold that boy Kal a four-hundrit dollar gat for fifteen- hundrit."

"What did you say?"

"You got to be jokin', yo. I had to give the man props. That was slick."

"I'm trying to get this straight, Freeze. After Scholar popped the bouncer at the Kiki, he sold Kal the murder weapon?"

"And make hisself a killin' on the dealy."

29

Sallie eyed Vooko without comment. The Bronx boy was dressed to impress and looking amazingly credible. He wore a navy Hugo Boss suit and a Dolce & Gabbana light blue shirt. If it weren't for the over-sized opal pimp ring on his index finger, he might have been mistaken for someone who had a steady day job. The lineup Sal ordered was ready and waiting for him. Six badass men, all about the same age, color and size as Scholar were standing with him under the lights.

Vooko took his time. Sal guessed from the blood lust avenger look on Vooko's face that the man was savoring his moment of retribution. Watching as Vooko sized up one man after the other, Sallie would later say the young man was in rapture.

"So, do you see the man who shot your cousin?"

Vooko was biting his lower lip. He had tears in his eyes. Sallie wondered if they were from rage, sadness or both. With a deliberate movement, Vooko pointed to the second man from the left. It was Scholar.

"That is the man who shot my cousin."

"Thank you, Vooko," Sallie said, shaking his hand. "I'm going to have you make a statement and then you're free to go home. And stay out of trouble."

Vooko looked as the men in the lineup left the room. "Thank you detective," he said, then gave Sal something hugely unexpected. A hug.

After watching Vooko leave with the officer, Sallie flipped a few cards on his Rolodex, and then dialed the Mamaroneck police chief, Phil Constanza. "Phil...Sal here."

"Sallie. How ya doin'? I was just about ready to give you a shout."

"Oh yeah. I hope it's good news."

"It's a match."

"Wow."

"The bullets fired from the gun that whacked the kid in Manhattan matched the one that killed Donny Donovan."

Sallie's mind went into overdrive. "You got any ideas or witnesses, Phil?"

"Nobody up here saw anything."

"How about from the crime scene?"

"We found several different types of hair in Donovan's bed, both pubic and head. I'm assuming all but Donny's are from females, but we haven't found out who the lucky girls were. Also, the stud was pumped with steroids. The ME said the stuff we found in his kitchen was hospital quality. If you'd like, I can send you what I've got."

"Thanks, Phil. I'd appreciate it as soon as you can." Sallie stared out the dirty office window for a full five minutes, all the while picking almonds from his molars. Then he reached over and pushed the bag of the remaining nuts into his desk-side wastebasket.

Sallie reentered the interrogation room. Scholar was tapping his foot like a maniac, way stressed. "I've got some bad news, Scholar," Sal said, sliding onto the chair opposite him. "I've now got *two* witnesses who will testify that they saw *you* kill the bouncer, Pashko, last Saturday night."

"Okay, yo. Have it your way. I did it. I killed that boy in self-defense."

Sallie wagged his head. "Am I hearing you correctly? You're saying that you're the shooter, Scholar?"

"Whatever."

"Then...let me get that straight. That Kessler kid *didn't* pay *you* to do the deed?"

"Man, how could that be, when I just tolt you it was done in self-defense?"

Sallie scratched his cheek. "Maybe because you needed to come up with fifteen-thousand dollars to make a demo."

Scholar cast his eyes to the ground. "Whatever."

"Okay, so you killed Pashko in self-defense. *Then* you sold Kal the gun."

"No."

"But you told me you sold him the gun."

"No, man. I lied."

"But, I have witnesses who told me you sold him the gun."

"They seriously mistaken."

Sallie had to hand it to Scholar. He was one of the slickest characters he had ever come across. "I'm sure you know that we found the gun you say *you* used to kill Pashko in self-defense. It was on Kal Kessler."

"Word?"

"Are you going to tell me you smoked Pashko and then just handed the gun over to Kal?"

"I might of. I ain't sayin' nothin' else."

Suddenly, the door behind Sallie opened and a man with a fat face, a salt and pepper beard and curly grey thinning hair hustled into the room and over to Scholar. Murray Plotkin. Sallie's eyes widened. No fuckin' way. Pound for pound, he was New York City's most effective criminal lawyer. Scholar wasn't blowing smoke up Sal's ass on his own. He had been doing it on Plotkin's advice. And how could piss-poor Scholar afford the counsel of big-bucks Plotkin? He couldn't unless Plotkin was taking charity cases, and Sallie knew that Plotkin was strictly a play-if-you-pay guy.

"Good morning, Detective Messina. Have you been questioning my client without his attorney present?" Plotkin spoke in a straight from Canarsie accent in a high voice that made nails on a chalkboard seem as smooth as light jazz.

"Mr. Plotkin," Sallie said and shook his hand. They knew each other from "back in the day" when Sallie was an undercover cop. Back then, Plotkin was a prosecutor for the city. After ten years of shopping at low end outlets, he'd decided he wanted to move up to Bergdorfs. The move required money and there was no way he was going to get much of that unless he switched sides, which he did. The attorney became a deadly effective and expensive legal representative to New York's big money maggots. Looking at the slob in the world's most expensive threads was causing the detective gastric distress below and heartburn above. And he also felt fucked because he knew who he was up against.

"Good to see you again, detective. You're looking well." "I'm rather surprised to see you in our humble house on

a Saturday morning, counselor. Am I correct in assuming that this young man seated before me has you as his legal advisor?"

"You are correct, officer. I'm going to be representing Mr. Johnson." He placed his hand on Scholar's shoulder.

"I had no idea Mr. Johnson had the sort of money you charge your clients."

"Who needs money when you've got friends in high places?"

Sallie smiled, and in his best Truman Capote imitation said, "Thank you for clarifying things. I deplore it when things are not perfectly logical." Scholar, was sitting there like the cat that ate the canary. "Why don't you pull up that chair in the corner and we'll continue our chat," Sallie glanced at the two-way mirror. Even with the captain and his partners on the other side of it, he felt isolated and alone. The legendary Plotnick intimidated him. In a rarely used almost apologetic tone the detective continued. "We were discussing the fact that I have two witnesses who identified Mr.

Johnson—Scholar, as I'm used to calling him— as the killer of Pashko Gazivoda."

"It was self-defense, as I understand it." Plotkin said.

Sallie glanced at Scholar. "You're sticking with that story now?"

Scholar glanced at Plotkin.

Plotkin spoke for him. "That's what Mr. Johnson said happened, detective."

Sallie continued. "We also have the matter of Kal Kessler's gun. We have information that your client sold it to him." He turned to Scholar. "*Did you sell Kal Kessler the gun?*"

"No, I did not."

"So...my information is incorrect?"

"Correct." Scholar grinned.

"I believe he has something else he wants to add to that," Plotkin said.

With Plotkin strategizing for Scholar, Sal was expecting something magnificently devious, but he was still surprised by its magnitude when the punk from Far Rock said, "I did that lawyer upstate."

The new gold standard for the all-time high of lowlife, scumbag originality had just been set. When he recovered enough to grasp the ramifications of what he'd been told, he said, "Scholar am I hearing correctly? Are you telling me you were the one who shot the lawyer in Mamaroneck?"

Scholar glanced at Plotkin who nodded matter-of- factly. Then the prisoner affirmed with a note of triumph, "Correct."

Sallie smiled, then very amicably took the hand of the pugnacious lawyer. "We're finished for the day. It's always nice to see you, Murray. Wish that you were still playing for the good guys." To the hip-hop impresario/ wannabe, he waved a satirically dramatic "ave atque vale" meaning, "I've had enough, you degenerate piece of shit. Farewell."

30

L eah looked like she'd been crying. The rims of her eyes were swollen and red. "I'm sorry to bother you at a time like this, Miss Kessler. I know you're grieving over the untimely death of your brother, but I have a job to do. I'm sure you understand."

Sallie walked through the doorway. Nothing had changed since he'd been there earlier in the week. The place was still a wreck and if he weren't mistaken, the Diet Pepsi can he left on the coffee table was still there.

"Would you mind if I sit, Ms. Kessler?"

She led him into the living room. He took a seat in a familiar chair.

"Have you ever been to a wrestling match?"

"Are you joking, detective? What the fuck are you talking about? You came here to ask me that at a time like this?"

"I'm sorry I should have been more specific. Have you ever seen Donny wrestle?"

She looked panicked, her eyes darted from side to side, she tapped her leg frantically. "I don't believe I've had the pleasure."

Sallie noticed the black sneakers and pointed to them. "Prada?"

"Yeah," She said proudly.

"Would you mind if I take a look in your closets."

"Yes, I would very much."

"Okay." Sallie allowed his next question to wait. He wanted her to feel the weight of the silence.

She pouted her lips and grimaced, then pulled back her hair.

"You were wearing a mask," he continued. "You stayed in the room about a minute. What were you doing in the room, Ms. Kessler?"

Leah abruptly stood up, walked into the kitchen and got some water from the tap. She didn't offer any to Sallie.

"Please sit down, Ms. Kessler."

When she returned to the living room, tears were running down her face. She fell dramatically back on the coach.

"You were there watching a wrestling match between your father and Donny."

"It was disgusting. I had to leave."

"Why was it disgusting, Ms. Kessler?"

"How would you like to see your father wrestling in a leather mask? It was creepy. And the two of them were so vicious." The tears kept coming. Her lips trembled.

"How about Kal? What was Kal like?"

"He was sweet. He loved me. A lot."

"How did he and Donny get along?"

"Not very well."

"Did he and Donny ever fight?"

She started tapping her foot again and clutched a pillow tightly with both hands. "They yelled a lot."

"About what?"

"You name it. Anything. Lately it was about drugs. Kal was doing way too much and Donny kept telling him to get help."

"What did Kal say?"

"Kal told him to mind his own business."

"How about a car. Did they ever fight about a car?"

"Not that I know of."

"How about Donny's Lincoln? Do you know that car?"

"Donny had a Lincoln?"

"Come on, Ms. Kessler. This is a murder investigation I'm conducting. Please don't make me arrest you. Did Donny have a Lincoln?"

"Yes."

"Did he ever let Kal use it?"

Leah was trembling all over now.

"Leah, did Kal ever use it?"

"Fuck you, detective! Why don't you tell me?" She threw her head into the pillow and sobbed. Sal took off his jacket and put it on her like a blanket. Once she was all cried out, he went to the kitchen and filled a glass with water. While he was there he had some straight from the tap, then rubbed some on his face and the back of his neck. He then brought in the drink to Leah along with a paper towel that she used to wipe her tears away.

"I have a witness who saw Kal hit a bouncer from Kiki with the car. He also saw you get out and dial 911."

Leah had a surprised look on her face.

"So, your brother hit this kid. I assume it was intentional to get back at him for the fight they had at the Kiki."

"I told Kal to forget about it. But he wouldn't."

"Now tell me what happened after that."

"Kal dropped me off at my place and I went up to Mamaroneck to see Donny."

"And what about Kal?"

"He told me that he was going out to Far Rockaway to score."

"Okay, so you go up to Mamaroneck and he goes out to Far Rock. Right, then what happens?"

"That's it. End of story."

"Leah, what happens the next day?"

"Kal comes over, really early in the morning. He's completely stoned. He's got a gun. Donny says, 'What's up with the gun, Kal?' Kal's like, 'I just bought it, Donny. I need to crash.' Donny says 'How's the car?' Kal says, 'I had a little bit of an accident, but I'll get it fixed.'

"What kind of state was Donny in when he found out your brother'd wrecked his car?"

"Crazy. He'd been using steroids to bulk up. I think they were making him nuts."

"So what did he do?"

"He ran outside, checked the damage and came back in."

"Then what?"

"He told me to take my brother into a guest room, which I did. When I got back, he was on the phone screaming for my father to get up to Mamaroneck."

"Did he go?"

"Yeah, he was up within an hour. Donny was yelling at him, screaming really."

"About what?"

"Something about how fucked he was if Donny used his car and got into an accident, and how dad had to take Donny to the police and report it."

"Dad was like, no way Donny. We can work it out. Donny kept insisting. He said he was tired of the whole fucking family and dad should take Kal and his little girl and get the fuck out. I was like, 'Donny you can't mean that, I love you.' He was like 'Leah, you don't love anybody but yourself.' "

"What did your father do?"

"He asked me where Kal was. Then he went to get him."

"And what did you do?"

"I was crying. Begging Donny to take back the terrible things he had just said. But, he kept getting more angry and saying more horrible things."

"And your dad?"

"Dad shot him."

"He shot him?"

The woman was now full on hysterical and words were shooting out of her mouth. "Yeah, then he told me to get my brother and drive back to New York in his car. He said Donny would be okay. But Donny died, and then my dad wanted Kal to take the blame. Oh my god! Oh my god. Oh my god."

"What did your dad tell him?"

"He told Kal that, given his drug problems, he'd never spend time in jail."

"Kal believed that?"

She was rocking in a seated position, still clutching the pillow. "No. No. I don't think so. It was so sad." She rolled into a fetal position where she continued speaking through her jerky sobs. "He practically begged me to talk to dad and try to convince him to not make Kal do it."

"Did you try to talk your father out of it?"

Leah started to wail. "I never did. I never did. I'm so pathetic. God, I hate him."

"Where's your father now, Leah?"

"He's downstairs in Kal's apartment."

31

The detectives could not have pounded any louder. When no one answered, they kicked the door in unison and it blew open.

"Anybody home? Police! Anybody home?" Sal called. When he didn't get a response, he told the men to split up. Sal took the master bedroom.

"Black Sallie Blue Eyes. Come in." Sheldon Kessler lay on a king size bed, watching golf on one of the largest televisions Sal had ever seen.

"You're under arrest, Mr. Kessler."

"What for, Messina?" His eyes stayed on the screen.

"For the murder of Donny Donovan."

"That's good, detective, but highly speculative."

"You were going to let your son spend time in jail for something you did."

"Detective, my son was a selfish, useless, worthless kid who gave me nothing but headaches from the day he was born."

"He was your son."

"Shit."

"Why'd you kill your lawyer buddy?"

"I didn't kill anyone, detective."

A commercial for the new Lexus came on. Sheldon turned the tv off. "I'm going into the kitchen, detective. Can I offer you something to drink?"

"No thanks, I'm good."

"Of course, you're good, Messina."

The real estate mogul walked into the kitchen where Ted and Jackie were waiting. "Hello, detectives. It's nice of you to join us. Can I get you anything to drink?"

Sal's partners declined.

"Sit down, please. Make yourselves comfortable on the couch."

Kessler was moving and speaking very slowly, maybe even sedated, Sal thought.

He poured himself a coke from a can into a cut glass tumbler, then opened the freezer and threw some ice cubes in. When he came into the living room he had his drink in one hand and a gun in the other, pointed at Sallie.

"Tell me, Mr. Detective, why do you think I killed Donny?"

Sallie crossed his legs and leaned back confidently. Teddy and Jackie remained motionless.

"I think that you've been telling yourself you killed him to protect your family. He was going to report Kal to the police and Kal would be found guilty of assault with a vehicle. The time and place of the assault would put him at the scene of the murder in which he was implicated and that would be the end of him. So you shot him and left him to bleed to death."

Sheldon nodded, his gun hand rock steady.

"But this is what I really think. You wanted Donny dead for a long time. You hated him for all the things he was that you aren't, especially because your daughter loved him and you couldn't stand that."

"That's it, Dr. Freud?"

"Well to tell you the truth, it's not a pretty picture. A man who shoots his friend, lets him die and blames the shooting on his son is one cold son of a bitch." Kal sat up. "So what are you going to do now, shoot me?"

Kessler raised the gun.

"Kessler, you're not gonna shoot me. You shoot me and you're a dead man. You love yourself too much for that."

At that, Sal walked across the room until he stood right in front of the gun. As Kessler opened fire, Ted and Jackie fired three rounds each into him. His body rocked in spastic motion with each ferocious impact.

32

Sallie's ears are ringing so much from the blast of Kessler's gun, he can't hear Jackie and Ted screaming at him. They're moving their mouths, their bodies too, but everything is instant replay slow-mo. In the eternity before they reach him, he's hit the floor, hands over his ears. Now he's in a fetal position. The smell of Kessler's burnt flesh is nauseating. The smoke from the barrage of weapons lingers in the air, causing his eyes to tear.

"I'm okay," he says, "let me be. I'll be fine. Go check on Kessler." He uncurls and rolls on his back. He feels the blood surging through his body at high speed. He begins to deep breathe.

Kessler's face as he remembered it before the shot was fired seemed relaxed, resigned, without apparent anger or angst. Or was it? Now Sallie can't be sure. He is certain of how wrong he was in that moment of truth, and is consumed by guilt. Perhaps he'd been too involved emotionally to be dispassionate. Maybe the loathing he felt for the mogul caused him to misjudge. Clearly he never saw the set-up as Kessler staged his own demise.

"He's dead, Sal."

"Okay, call the captain. Let him know what happened."

Sal, in a state of shock, moves to a room with a desk. He's on a chair with a phone to his ear.

"Maury."

"Sal? What's up?"

"Maury, do you believe that evil exists?"

"Sal, give me a minute, I'm not hearing you too well, my wife has some of the family over. I need to go someplace quiet." Sal looks at the gaping hole in the ground across the street while he waits. Tears well up in his eyes.

"Okay, Sal. I'm back."

"Maury, do you believe that evil exists?" He asks again, voice trembling.

"I believe that people commit evil acts."

"And you defend them. You switched sides. Why?" He is pleading.

"I do not defend the act, Sal, I defend them. There's a big difference. I used to want to punish people, Sal. I really did."

"Now?"

"I want to give people the opportunity to change."

"Has anyone ever changed?"

"Yes, some have. What about you. Sal, do you believe evil exists?"

Sal begins to sob unabashedly. Across the street, machines are moving the scorched earth that many consider hallowed ground. Hopeful messages for peace and love are bound to a temporary fence surrounding it. "I know it does," he is struggling for words. And I know it can never be completely eradicated. But my job is to contain it by apprehending people who do bad things and prevent them from ever doing them again."

"And contrition and redemption?"

"That's for priests, Maury. It's a different business." Sal laughs and Plotkin joins him.

"Kessler's dead, Maury."

"Yeah?"

"He shot at me, and my guys killed him."

"He shot at you. Did he hit you? Are you hurt?"

"No. The fucker missed intentionally."

"Maybe it was his way of checking out. The last few days he was going on and on about how he didn't want to live anymore."

"What about the kid from the PJ's? You still going to represent him?"

"I don't think so, Sal. Sheldon was footing the bill. With him gone, your perp is pretty much on his own." Plotkin stayed silent for a while, a minor miracle. "Sal, I've heard cops say it over and over again. At first you want to get into the job, then the job gets into you. Know what I'm saying."

"I do Maury. I very much do. Thanks."

"God bless you, Sal."

33

Was it deference or nerves that caused Scholar to stand up when he entered? Sal couldn't tell. "What are you standing for? I'm not the fucking Queen, Scholar. Sit down."

Scholar sat back down as Sallie took the chair next to him. "You're fucked, Scholar. It's over. Sheldon Kessler's dead." The detective looked right at him in a way that was not without compassion.

"Why you wanna bullshit me like that?"

"I'm not bullshitting, Scholar. Believe me, I wish I were.
He was shot a little while ago."

"Oh yeah?"

"Yeah. He fired at me, and my partners took him out. I just got off the phone with Plotnick, he's not going to be working your case. It's going to the public defender."

"Word?"

"I give you my word."

Scholar leaned over, put his hand on his chin, elbow on his knee.

"Look, nothing you say here is gonna be recorded, you can tell the PD whatever the fuck you want. This is between us. Why'd you kill that young man?"

"Like I said before, you one tenacious motherfucker." Scholar smiled then sat up and leaned back.

"Come on. I really need to know."

"Why you think?"

"Scholar, if I knew, I wouldn't be asking."

"Ya know what I like about you, detective? I believe that you really do want to know."

"So what?"

"I ain't sayin' I did it, but I will say this. Imagine all your life you believe in your core that nothing matters, nothing you do, nothing you say, will ever amount to shit. Everything you see on TV, in the movies, read about in the paper is sending you a message saying be like me, buy what I buy, wear what I wear, act like I act. But you ain't them and you can't be. The reality that they're selling is so different from yours, you might as well be living in an another alternate type reality. No man, scratch that shit, you are living in a different reality.

"Their reality is chock fulla white people and is predicated on the assumption that you understand their ways. Your reality does not include white people and as for understanding what they're about, let's be real, how you gonna do, if you don't know any? Their reality is loaded with college-educated people making legit money, and folks with decent jobs that got new cars, nice lawns and clean driveways. Your reality is filled with drugs, high school dropouts, welfare, and section 8 housing. So that shit they selling you 24/7, you ain't got a clue how to get it but you know having it means you somebody.

"You burnin' up inside. Say to yourself, 'Somebody recognize me. Tell me I'm someone. Better yet, don't tell me, show me." But nobody ain't telling you nothin', 'cause you ain't exceptional. You ain't no athlete, you ain't got great music in you, you ain't funny, an A student or super motivated. No, man, you just a normal everyday ordinary motherfucker, but not really, because in the their reality, everyday ordinary motherfuckers, these non-exceptional people, graduate from school, get jobs and eventually get a crib, a car and like that.

"So one day I akse myself, Scholar what they got that you ain't got? I marinate on it for days 'til it finally comes. They got a dream, something that matters to them. See, since I don't believe in nothin' I ain't gonna get nothin'.

"Look, man, I ain't blind. I see immigrants come to this country and in a few years they living good. And I ain't talking 'bout just white folks. I see brothers from Africa and Haiti movin' up like. Why ain't I? Because I ain't got a dream.

"See without this dream, what am I gonna do? I'm gonna get me trouble. But you know what, I'm so damn fucked up, I'll take it and pretend it's something I wanted all along.

"But hey, I think it's in a man's nature to dream 'cause I had one when I see the brothers on the MTV rockin' the other reality with a hip-hop beat and a lifestyle that they was embracing. That's right, I had a dream. So I tried to make it happen. You can't blame a man for doing what he do to make his dream into reality, can you?"

"So you shot the guy at the Kiki." Sal said matter-of- factly.

Scholar shook his head. "Motherfucker, is that all that you got to say to what I just be telling you? Shit, man, you don't have a clue. Where's my lawyer? I need to get me the fuck out of here."

Epilogue

With Sheldon dead, there was no one around to foot his legal expenses, so Scholar was left with an overworked public defender to plead his case. Net/net, Scholar went up for a hard twenty-five.

And Freeze, Pea Head and Science, fuck those pussy motherfuckers! Last time Scholar heard, Pea Head was a youth counselor. Do you believe that shit? And Science, he was scraping by as a security guard, working the graveyard shift at a private hospital in Queens.

Freeze, the motherfucker who ratted his ass away? Man, Freeze was dead, serves the no-good brotha right. A couple of Jamaican dealers caught up with him after he beat them on a drug deal. Them Rastas man, they as bad as those Aryan Nation motherfuckers, best to give them a wide berf, everybody know that don't nobody want to mess with them, yo. They bury your sorry ass without mercy, for real. What was that fool Freeze thinkin'?

Meanwhile, Vooko sits in his favorite seat at the diner looking at a copy of the paper while he waits for an international repast of Canadian bacon, French toast, and Colombian coffee.

The headline's ALL IN THE FAMILY, the picture is of a stunningly chic young woman getting into a limo. Five inside pages are devoted to different takes on the Kessler family woes, including a two-page spread with a detailed time line of Kal's altercation with Vooko, Scholar's hit for hire, Kal's hit and run and the sordid facts surrounding the Donny Donovan murder.

Page four features an old close-up of a smiling Sallie, blue eyes twinkling. The headline above is IT'S OVER.

Below is a recap of the unprovoked assault by the megalomaniac, Sheldon Kessler. The story goes on to report the details leading to his violent death. Below it is another photo of the Detective Messina. The caption reads, "Detective Salvadore Messina, aka Black Sallie Blue Eyes, the man who cracked the case."

Between bites he studies Leah, what a dime. He feels her in a big way. Hey man, you got to have some sympathy. She couldn't help it if she was the sister of the little prick that was the cause of so much unnecessary grief. She was more like a victim. Selfish pops, phony-ass moms, whack-ass bro, where was the love in that family? Fuck it. What's done is done. Best be putting it behind.

Right now, Vooko's got his mind on other things, productive ones. His uncle, for one, and how he had bought a couple of old brownstones in Fort Greene that he had did over. They was nice. The kind of residences that appeal to folks who can't pay five million dollars for a Manhattan brownstone—but even though they always be poor-mouthing, they still have more money than ninety- nine percent of the rest of the people living on the planet. Vooko can see that it's a way for a smalltime guy to make some big- time dinero, in a relatively short amount of time, so he's signed on to learn the ropes by doing grunt work for his uncle's latest project, a renovation in Greenpoint. He got a dream, yo, and he's keeping his eyes on the prize: a smokin' crib south of the highway, check it out, there's a picture of it posted on the front window of Sotheby's real estate office in East Hampton. No price is given.

Another Sunday night of basketball at Chelsea Piers is over. Sallie scores a new record high for himself—twenty- five points, ten from the outside, eight driving to the hoop, and seven from the line. As soon as gets home, he takes a couple of Advil to preempt the pain. The play had been physical, anyone challenging the defense inside the paint paid a heavy price.

After a long hot shower, he lies down on the couch and turns the tv on. Six hundred channels and he can't find one that holds his attention. He hits the remote. Off the big screen goes, and when it does the room is a New York City dark, where the night sky still has a soft electric glow.

The phone rings.

"Sal?" It's Donna.

"Yep."

"Sal, I'm sorry. I should have never invited you."

He thinks about the slow dance at the Waldorf, and starts to feel a little of the giddiness he felt before the night got ugly. Forgiveness never has been in his makeup. In the line of work he's chosen, there's little evidence that it leads to anything but repeat performances of social deviance. Still he forces himself to stay on the line while he both acknowledges this empirical truth and looks for strength to transcend it. He flashes on the conversation with Maury Plotnick.

"Sure, I forgive you. We all do regrettable things, Donna. It doesn't make us bad people." With that said, he feels unburdened, light, clean, hopeful, redeemed.

Acknowledgments

Many thanks to my editors Marianne Rogoff, Michael Carr, Michael Denneny, and Nancy O. Johanson for their patience, encouragement and expertise, and to Brian del Fiore for introducing me to Michael. Much gratitude to my agent Barbara Lowenstein, for always having me covered, to Tim Schaffner, editor and publisher, who helped me take this book Next Level and continues to inspire, coach, and believe.

Big love to my wife Jeanne, our daughters Hayley, Heartie, and Hannnah, Ken Kalfus, Peter DeJonge, Jack Livesy, Yehuda Nir, Ori Brafman, Dr. Penny Donnenfeld, The Shannon-Donnenfelds, David and Lisa Blatte, Dr. Nancy Brockington, David Hall, Lynne Neary, Joanne Mackenzie, John Kelly, Rob Malkin, Deb Lucke, Paul Hartzel, Tom Hammond, Arlene Harrison, Dr. Bob Sammartano, Tom and Camille Gambale, Larry Gottlieb, JB Moore, Skip Whitman, Brad Worrell for the immense support. To the playas, hustlers, gangsters, ballers, producers, and street geniuses, for the good, the bad and the ugly back in the day of Mighty Music.

Special thanks to NYPD Detective Tom Nerny, Homicide South for passing along the expression Humpty Dumpty Was Pushed and introducing me to NYPD police protocol. You are a sage and a saint. Respect and admiration goes to the Thirteenth Precinct Detectives William A. Hamilton Andrew Jackson, John C Banville, John J.Vergona, and Lt. Michael Walsh.

Made in the USA
Coppell, TX
24 June 2021